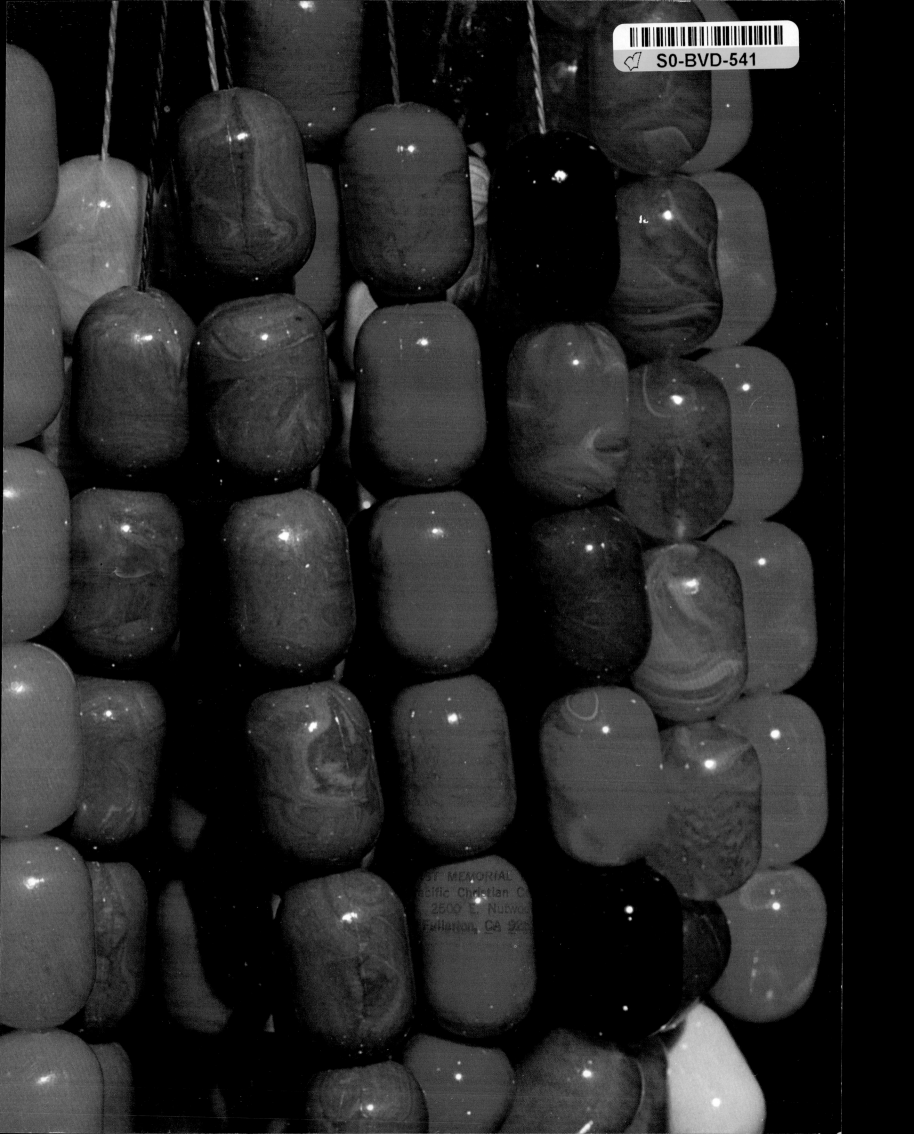

ATHENS

By William Wyatt Davenport
and the Editors of Time-Life Books

With Photographs by Constantine Manos
and Michael Freeman

THE GREAT CITIES · TIME-LIFE BOOKS · AMSTERDAM

The Author: William Wyatt Davenport was born in New York and educated at Columbia University and at the University of Paris. A frequent magazine contributor, he has also written a number of travel books, including *India: A Personal Guide.* He first went to Athens, as a student, in 1936 and has returned there many times during the past four decades. He has lived in France since 1957 and, as director of Northwood Institute Europe, he supervises academic programmes for American students in Paris, Vicenza and Athens.

The Photographers: Born in South Carolina, Constantine Manos began working as a photographer at the age of 15. In 1964 he joined Magnum Photos, an international agency. His book, *A Greek Portfolio*, published in 1972, won awards at the Arles and Leipzig Book Fairs. He has held exhibitions in Europe and the United States, and is also represented in the permanent collection of the Museum of Modern Art in New York City.

Michael Freeman was born in England and launched his photographic career in 1971 with an exhibition of pictures taken during a trip up the Amazon River. He has contributed to a number of leading British and European magazines, including *Vogue* and West Germany's *Geo* magazine.

TIME-LIFE INTERNATIONAL
EUROPEAN EDITOR: George Constable
Assistant European Editor: Kit van Tulleken
Design Consultant: Louis Klein
Chief Designer: Graham Davis
Director of Photography: Pamela Marke

THE GREAT CITIES
Editorial Staff for Athens
Editors: John Cottrell, Christopher Farman
Designers: Derek Copsey, Eric Molden
Picture Editor: Jasmine Spencer
Staff Writers: Tony Allan, Mike Brown
Text Researchers: Elizabeth Loving, Milly Trowbridge
Design Assistants: Steve Duwensee, Fiona Preston

Editorial Production
Production Editor: Ellen Brush
Art Department: Julia West
Editorial Department: Joanne Holland, Ajaib Singh Gill
Picture Department: Lynn Farr, Gina Marfell

The captions and the texts accompanying the photographs in this volume were prepared by the editors of TIME-LIFE Books.

Published by TIME-LIFE International (Nederland) B.V.
Ottho Heldringstraat 5, Amsterdam 1018.

© 1978 TIME-LIFE International (Nederland) B.V.
All rights reserved. First printing in English.

No part of this book may be reproduced in any form or by any electronic or mechanical means, including information storage and retrieval devices or systems without prior written permission from the publisher, except that brief passages may be quoted for reviews.

Valuable assistance was given in the preparation of this volume by the TIME Correspondent in Athens, Dean Brelis, and his assistant, Mirka Gondicas, and also by the TIME-LIFE Correspondent in Rome, Ann Natanson.

Cover: Scarred Corinthian columns of the Temple of Olympian Zeus, completed more than 1,800 years ago, form an incongruous grid with the balconies of a modern apartment block in central Athens. Only 15 of the temple's original 104 columns still stand.

First end paper: Strings of multi-coloured, plastic "worry beads" dangle in a shop display. Known as *komboloia*, they serve as trinkets for Greek men, who finger them obsessively at times of idleness or tension.

Last end paper: Fragments of stone from ancient buildings lie strewn on an archaeological site near the 2nd-Century ruins of Hadrian's Library, in the Plaka district of Athens.

THE TIME-LIFE ENCYCLOPAEDIA
OF GARDENING
HUMAN BEHAVIOUR
THE GREAT CITIES
THE ART OF SEWING
THE OLD WEST
THE WORLD'S WILD PLACES
THE EMERGENCE OF MAN
LIFE LIBRARY OF PHOTOGRAPHY
FOODS OF THE WORLD
TIME-LIFE LIBRARY OF ART
GREAT AGES OF MAN
LIFE SCIENCE LIBRARY
LIFE NATURE LIBRARY
YOUNG READERS LIBRARY

Contents

I

The Glorious Survivor

"What I desire is that you fix your eyes every day on the greatness of Athens and fall in love with her. . . . Mighty indeed are the marks and monuments of our empire which we have left. Future ages will wonder at us, as the present age wonders at us now." These words were addressed to Athenians by the great general and statesman Pericles in the year 432 B.C., when the city-state he led could boast colonies and tribute-paying allies from as far afield as Sicily in the west and the Black Sea in the east. Today, more than 2,400 years later, tourists from all over the world descend on the capital of Greece at the rate of some three million annually—almost every one of them resolved to fix their eyes on the monumental relics of that greatness.

My own passion for Athens has now lasted for almost half a century. My father read Homer's *Iliad* and *Odyssey* to me as bedtime stories, and I was thoroughly addicted to Greek mythology from the age of six. I found the rape of Europa more interesting than Rumpelstiltskin, and the riotous high life of the gods on Mount Olympus more appealing than the heavy pronouncements of Hebrew prophets. On my bedroom wall was a photograph of history's most celebrated *déjà vu*, etched on the retina of every civilized eye: the Acropolis. I could hardly wait to see the real thing.

I finally achieved my ambition in 1936, at the end of my freshman year at New York's Columbia University, during which my boyhood addiction had been deepened by a compulsory course: *Humanities I* (the required reading for it included Pindar, Thucydides, Aeschylus, Sophocles, Euripides, Aristophanes, Socrates, Plato, Aristotle—all of them street names of modern Athens). That summer I made a pilgrimage to the city that had nurtured these men. At the first possible opportunity I ascended the Acropolis, the 512-foot-high rock citadel of the ancient capital, and found myself gazing at the Parthenon and other ruins in a philhellenic trance.

In classical times, all Athenian religious and civic life revolved around this sacred rock, sanctuary of Athena, Goddess of Wisdom. It was the epicentre of an intellectual and cultural explosion whereby Athens of the 5th and 4th Centuries B.C. influenced Western civilization to a greater extent than any other city on earth.

The sense of history was overwhelming. On the oval plateau of the Acropolis, I looked out from the natural fortress that had served cave-dwellers—the first Athenians—in the 7,000-year-old darkness of the Neolithic Age. On the terrain in its shadow, I could see where democracy was born, sit where the first great plays were performed, walk where great

An early morning mist, laden with marble-corroding pollutants, laps around the Acropolis —the central plateau where ancient Athenians built their temples. The monuments are endangered by their own fame as well as by air pollution: millions of tourists visit the Acropolis each year and, with the vibrations of footsteps, are undermining the foundations of the shrines.

philosophers endlessly walked and talked, stand where St. Paul stood to preach his new religion.

All around me, ancient history abounded, freed from the cobwebs of the classical textbooks I had recently been studying and thereby given a dramatic new dimension. It was easy to observe the wish of Pericles: to fall in love with so much splendour in marble and wonder at the greatness of his Athens. But then I looked beyond the ruins and fixed my eyes on the urban chaos of modern Athens, burgeoning at breakneck speed without any cohesiveness of style or taste. This modern city, I thought, could never be loved at first sight. On the contrary, the strongest emotion I felt at that moment was deep dismay.

Many years and many visits later, I find myself even more aware of the conflict between the best of things ancient and the worst of things modern. Regrets are inescapable, since Athens was endowed with a physical setting that any city might envy. The Acropolis and a second peak, Mount Lycabettus, rise at the heart of the central, 170-square-mile plain of the Attic peninsula; on the eastern, northern and western edges of that plain stand protective mountains, ranging from 1,354 feet to 4,636 feet high; to the south-west lie the natural harbours and shimmering waters of the Saronic Gulf, gateway to the Aegean Sea and thence to the Mediterranean and the Black Sea.

Unfortunately, the city has taken on a vulgar, mid-20th-Century spread, occupying almost all of the plain with characterless cubes of concrete and brick. The once-brilliant, crystalline light is now blurred by fumes from traffic and factories; and the nearby waters are contaminated by sewage and industrial waste. Each time I return to Athens, I find that the city has been increasingly marred by disorderly expansion and cheapened further by such touristy trappings as pizza parlours, discothèques, strip clubs and clip-joints. Yet, miraculously, the intrinsic beauty of its setting still shines through its unbecoming, ultra-modern apparel. It still has tremendous visual impact, still qualifies as one of the most exciting and romantic cities on earth.

The Acropolis is, of course, the master key to any appreciation of Athens. This massive limestone citadel towers above the modern city and presents on its plateau and periphery the world's most spectacular concentration of great works of antiquity: the standing remains of three temples and a gateway that were constructed in the 5th Century B.C., and traces of at least seven other temples or shrines dating from the 6th to the 1st Centuries B.C. The plateau is the heart and soul and inspiration of the city, all in one—a centrepiece of such spellbinding grandeur that it illuminates the dreariest of quarters in the metropolis.

If you ask anyone who has visited Athens to describe his most magical memory of the city, you can be virtually certain that the Acropolis, directly or by association, will figure in the reply. The answer may be a recollection

After a visit with her children in Athens, an old woman sorrowfully looks back at the city from the rail of a ferry that will return her to her home on the island of Karpathos. Roughly two out of every three Athenians are immigrants from the Greek islands, remote mainland villages, or Asia Minor.

of dining out at a roof-garden restaurant with a view of the 2,400-year-old Parthenon (often called "the world's most perfect building") soaring triumphantly against the night sky; or watching a Greek tragedy unfold at the Odeon of Herodes Atticus, an 1,800-year-old white marble theatre nestling against the southern flank of the Acropolis. Alternatively, the visitor may cite the spectacular *Son et Lumière* on the Pnyx Hill where, each night in summer, the city's marble crown is flooded with the beams of 1,500 spotlights; remember an adventure in Plaka, the ancient *taverna*-packed quarter that tumbles down the north-east slope of the Acropolis in such a tangle of narrow streets and alleys that even Athenians lose their way; or perhaps recall taking a night-cap on the lofty parapet of Mount Lycabettus, a little over a mile from the Acropolis and some 300 feet higher, and seeing one of the most stunning sights on earth: the Aegean sunset turning the white marble of the Parthenon to brilliant gold.

Athens and the Acropolis are inseparable in the human experience. I know of no other city in the world that is so completely dominated, both physically and emotionally, by a single landmark. Financially, too, the sacred rock is of vital importance. It is the main pillar of a tourist industry that brings Greece nearly $1 billion a year, or roughly one-third of all its foreign exchange. The Acropolis represents the classical Athens that every schoolboy vaguely knows and every foreign visitor expects to see—a city of such breathtaking accomplishment that its very name has become synonymous with culture and learning. As Plutarch, the Greek essayist and biographer, observed of this citadel 19 centuries ago: "There is a sort of bloom of newness upon those works, preserving them from the touch of time, as if they had some perennial spirit and undying vitality mingled in the composition of them."

Perhaps so, but the Athens that surrounds those works appears hell-bent on self-destruction. This 20th-Century cosmopolis is jam-packed with almost three million citizens, about a third of the entire population of Greece, and it has no more room to breathe as it pushes up against the natural boundaries of mountains and sea. In spite of being named for the Goddess of Wisdom, the city is recklessly sacrificing itself to those twin deities, Commerce and Industry; and, in that process, it is creating traffic and pollution problems of such appalling proportions that they have become an environmentalist's nightmare.

Most foreigners instinctively think of Athens as an ancient metropolis. But apart from the Acropolis and its environs, the city has developed entirely in modern times—mostly in the past 60 years. Modern Athens is actually one of the *youngest* capitals in Europe; it is less than 150 years old, younger even than Washington D.C., seat of the United States government since the dawn of the 19th Century. True, in Pericles' day, Athens had been one of the most important cities in the Western world, but its early role as the centre of an empire was fleeting.

The so-called Golden Age of Athens extended only from 480-430 B.C. —half a century of power and prosperity that began with the against-all-odds rout of the Persian invaders at Salamis, just off the coast of Piraeus, and ended in the miseries of a great plague and a drawn-out war with the rival Greek city-state of Sparta. Thereafter, Athens never fully recovered her former position of power. Indeed, for more than two millennia, the city was to endure foreign intrusion: domination first by the Macedonians and later by the Romans; invasions by Goths, Franks and Venetians; and finally almost 400 years of Turkish domination. The Turks were ousted during the Greek War of Independence, which lasted from 1821 to 1829. But by then, once-mighty Athens was no more than an obscure, semi-feudal township of 6,000 residents and a few hundred rickety houses clinging to the north slope of the Acropolis. ("The least ruined objects here," an English visitor reported, "are some of the ruins themselves.")

Modern Athens dates from that time. The ramshackle town was reborn in 1834, when it was promoted—largely on the strength of its long-ago greatness—to the status of capital of the newly liberated nation of Greece. In December of that year, the reconstituted city had the dubious honour of welcoming the first monarch of Greece, a 19-year-old Bavarian prince who had been baptized as Otto and was now restyled Otho I. In Athens, King Otho moved into a two-storey house—the only one in town—and set his team of German architects working on plans for a palace and a new city to be centred on the fields north-west of the Acropolis.

A chaotic traffic jam chokes a street on the lower slopes of Mount Lycabettus. The number of vehicles in the city has trebled within a decade.

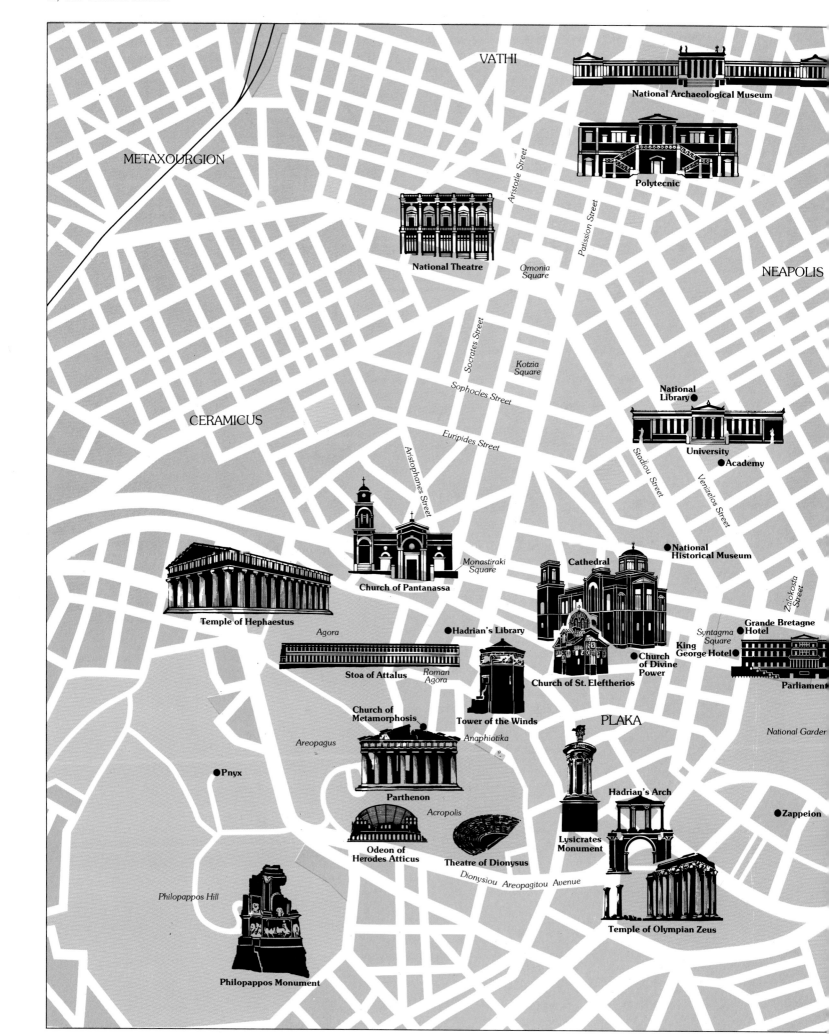

VATHI

METAXOURGION

NEAPOLIS

National Archaeological Museum

Polytecnic

Aristotle Street

Patission Street

National Theatre

Omonia Square

Socrates Street

Kotzia Square

Sophocles Street

CERAMICUS

Euripides Street

National Library ●

Stadiou Street

Venizelos Street

University

● **Academy**

Aristophanes Street

● **National Historical Museum**

Cathedral

Church of Pantanassa

Monastiraki Square

Zalokosta Street

Temple of Hephaestus

Agora

●**Hadrian's Library**

Grande Bretagne Hotel

Syntagma Square

Church of Divine Power

King George Hotel ●

Stoa of Attalus

Roman Agora

Church of St. Eleftherios

Parliament

Church of Metamorphosis

Tower of the Winds

PLAKA

Areopagus

Anaphiotika

●**Pnyx**

National Garden

Parthenon

Hadrian's Arch

● **Zappeion**

Acropolis

Lysicrates Monument

Odeon of Herodes Atticus

Theatre of Dionysus

Dionysiou Areopagitou Avenue

Philopappos Hill

Temple of Olympian Zeus

Philopappos Monument

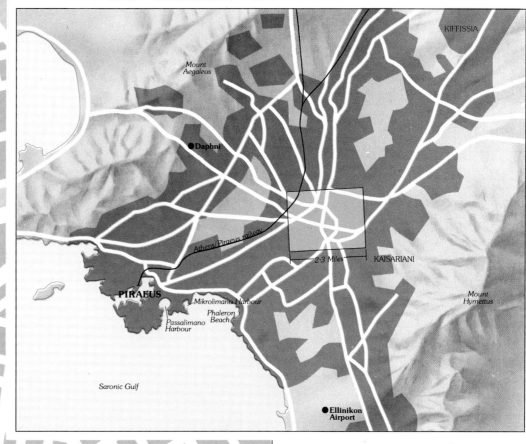

Marble-hearted Colossus

Athens, hardly more than a modest-sized town when it became the capital of Greece in 1834, now sprawls over almost 170 square miles of a peninsula jutting into the Aegean Sea. The ever-expanding suburbs of Greater Athens (inset map below) now include the thriving port of Piraeus, located five miles to the south-west of the city centre.

Broad avenues funnel into Omonia Square in the working-class area near the heart of the metropolis and into chic Syntagma Square further south. But the true focus of the city is the Acropolis, the central plateau crowned by a peerless complex of classical temples. Around its base, lies the Plaka district, containing other ancient monuments and ruins, along with a scattering of Byzantine churches. Mount Lycabettus, the National Gardens and public parks (green areas) provide open spaces for Athens' three million inhabitants.

Alexandras Avenue

Panathenaikos●
Soccer Stadium

Mount
Lycabettus
●St. George's Chapel
Funicular
railway

ndar Street

KOLONAKI

Kolonaki
Square

Benaki
●Museum

Vassilissis Sofias
Avenue

Byzantine Museum

●Royal Palace

Vassileos Constantinou Avenue

Mount
dettus

Stadium

KIFFISSIA

Mount
Aegaleos

●Daphni

Athens/Piraeus railway

2·3 Miles   KAISARIANI

PIRAEUS

Mikrolimano Harbour

Phaleron
Passalimano   Beach
Harbour

Mount
Hymettus

Saronic Gulf

●Ellinikon
Airport

At a kiosk in Piraeus, seaport suburb of Athens, business halts as soccer buffs gather to watch an important match on a television set provided by the owner.

Why should the Greeks choose a foreigner for their king? The answer is that they didn't. The choice had been made in London in 1832 by a conference of the statesmen of Britain, France and Russia. In 1827, the three great European powers had intervened militarily on behalf of the Greek freedom fighters, primarily out of self-interest and fear that the balance of power might be disturbed in a region of such strategic importance. Now, as self-appointed mediators, the "protecting powers" had endowed the new state with a hereditary monarchy based on their own choice of king. Otto, son of the philhellene King Ludwig of Bavaria, was a Roman Catholic and he spoke no Greek. He was strictly the choice of compromise and defensive thinking—a candidate acceptable to all parties and not affiliated to any significant faction in Greece.

King Otho reigned for almost 30 years. But Athens was not rapidly transformed by his arrival. Four years afterwards, a French visitor to the royal city wrote gloomily: "There are still no streets and the first work to be embarked on is a palace. . . . Everywhere it is a scene of demolition and construction side by side, a state of chaos where today's buildings are as flimsy as what collapsed yesterday. Briefly, everything in this poor town is either a rough sketch or else a ruin." Gradually, the sketch assumed substance; on the ruins of Turkish Athens rose a pleasant market town of modest proportions and neoclassical (so-called "Othonian") style, relying on considerable use of columns, pediments and porticos. Yet, well after the turn of the century, there was still no hint that Athens might become a great city of the modern world. By 1920, its population totalled fewer than 300,000—a mere 17 per cent of the national figure.

Since then, by way of mass intakes of refugees and migrants looking for work, Athens has swollen to a grotesque—some say unmanageable—size. Its spectacular, higgledy-piggledy growth began in 1922 after the Turks, led by Mustafa Kemal Atatürk, had repelled a Greek invasion of territories in Asia Minor under Turkish domination. To escape the ensuing massacre, thousands of Greeks fled across the Aegean Sea, and many of them landed at Piraeus, the port located five miles south-west of Athens.

The following year, under pressure from the Great Powers, the two warring nations accepted a peace settlement that gave Turkey the whole of Asia Minor, together with Constantinople and Eastern Thrace at the top of the Aegean, while Greece was awarded Western Thrace. This agreement also entailed an extraordinary "exchange of population"—400,000 Turks in Greece for 1,500,000 Greeks in Asia Minor. Many of those Greeks had to leave without any compensation for loss of property.

As a result of the great exchange, approximately 300,000 displaced persons settled in and around the Greek capital. A national census taken shortly thereafter revealed that Athens had a population of nearly 500,000, of whom less than 30 per cent were Athenians by birth. Two decades later, this disparity was accentuated as a second tidal wave of refugees swept over Athens and Piraeus—this time, mainland Greeks uprooted from towns and villages destroyed during the Second World War and the ensuing civil war between pro- and anti-Communist forces (the internal struggle lasted until 1949, when the Communists were defeated).

These new Athenians took advantage of a law that in effect conferred squatters' rights on anyone who overnight could put up four walls and a roof. Meanwhile, the civic authorities were too pre-occupied with civil conflicts and political rivalries to dwell on the intricacies of long-term city planning. In consequence, Athens expanded like a wild onion, taking on ring after ring of hastily built shanty towns—which were eventually replaced by artless slabs of concrete. Hillside greenery fast disappeared. There was no provision for parks and lakes, or even playground space for schools. Spreading seawards, the urban sprawl merged Athens with the industrial and commercial port of Piraeus; inland, it reached the limits set by the mountains of Parnes, Pentelicon, Hymettus and Aegaleos.

On approaching the city from the airport of Ellinikon to the south, the first-glance impression of present-day Athens is of a congealed sea of cement covering all the visible land from the mountains to the Saronic Gulf. From afar, thousands of white cement housing units, mostly two to seven storeys high, appear as so many tombstones densely packed together in a haphazard sprawl. In the heart of the city, 30 landscaped acres make up the attractive National Gardens. But this is a rare gem indeed. Only 3 per cent of Athens is devoted to parkland, making it the capital with the least greenery in Europe.

The approximate centre of modern Athens, just six miles north of the airport, is Syntagma (Constitution) Square, a broad plaza dominated on its eastern side by the former royal palace—a massive, fawn-coloured and shuttered building of totally undistinguished, neoclassical design. Young King Otho personally chose this site for his royal residence in 1834. According to popular legend, the most salubrious spot was selected by hanging hunks of meat in various parts of the ruined town and observing the place where maggots were slowest to hatch. I find this hard to believe, even in a city of miracles and myths. The location—almost exactly midway between the two great landmarks of central Athens, the Acropolis and Mount Lycabettus—is altogether too logical and precise to have been decided by the larvae of flies.

Syntagma is the hub of tourist Athens (the focus of the workaday city is Omonia Square, 12 blocks north-west). On the marble forecourt of the old palace, now the Parliament building, foreign visitors pose amid pigeons and click their cameras at the pleat-skirted Evzones (Presidential Guard) stationed on either side of the Tomb of the Unknown Soldier, dedicated to all Greeks fallen in war since the struggle for independence. On the south and west flanks, the square is rimmed by the offices of airlines, travel agencies and banks; on the north side, tower grand hotels: the King George, a veritable palace with its own picture gallery of 19th-Century Greek Masters, and the monumental Grande Bretagne, which served as German military headquarters during the Axis occupation.

In summer, almost 3,000 customers can be seated in the open-air cafés that spill on to Syntagma's sidewalks and range around the orange trees, parterres and fountains of its island centre. Here, hours become minutes for those who care to sit in idleness, sipping drinks, spearing melon slices and watching the passing parade: the élite of Athenian society arriving for a gala at the Grande Bretagne; macho Greeks on the prowl for unchaperoned girls; elderly sponge-pedlars festooned with their wares; lottery-sellers with their tickets flying like pennants on banner-style poles. Maybe, just maybe, you will see a run by the bravest men in Athens—the waiters from one of the great hotels who, with trays held aloft, sometimes slalom across a minefield of non-stop traffic to serve a special customer at a table on the square's central island.

Any aerial impression of Athens as a graveyard is totally destroyed on the ground, and most especially at this bustling square, the junction of main avenues carrying eight lanes of traffic. Here, as in Omonia Square, one feels closer to Indianapolis than to the Acropolis; this spot is a harrowing concourse for the ubiquitous god of modern Athenians—a honking, snarling metal minotaur that spews out noxious gases you can readily taste as well as smell. The city has about a quarter of a million private cars and nearly 12,000 taxis—more than half of all Greece's light motor transport—and it has been estimated that, together with the city's grubby blue buses (the worst offenders), they contribute 25 per cent of the 150,000 tons of sulphur dioxide scattered into the Athenian air every year.

In winter, the downtown streets are often so choked with traffic that walking is a far quicker way of getting about than driving. "Every day it is getting worse, and every year it will go on getting worse," a veteran Athenian cabbie said to me on my most recent visit, echoing a fatalistic attitude that I heard expressed again and again. (Like so many of his artful colleagues, he passionately advocated one "logical solution": ban all private cars from the streets.) In midsummer, when temperatures regularly nudge the 90s Fahrenheit, the traffic is lighter—just light enough for drivers to indulge their natural passion for speed (officially limited to 30 miles an hour in the city). Then, Athenians firmly establish themselves as being among the most aggressive and competitive drivers in Europe. Any pedestrian, any other car, qualifies as their quarry. Tailgating is a mark of courage; to be passed by another car is an unendurable affront.

The screeching of brakes, the blaring of horns, the squeal of hot rubber cornering on concrete—these are the most familiar sounds in central Athens, a cacophony often accompanied by the thundering of pneumatic drills and occasionally punctuated by a collision of car bumpers and a lively

The 2,400-year-old Acropolis temples loom beyond Monastiraki Square's later shrines—a 10th-Century church (left) and an 18th-Century mosque (centre).

exchange of obscenities. The roar of traffic never stops. At 2 a.m., I have sat at Zonar's Café on Venizelos Street, directly north of Syntagma Square, and watched cars racing by as though matched in their own Olympic grand prix. Where do they come from? Where do they go? Even though petrol is fearfully expensive in Athens, I cannot escape the feeling that these compulsive charioteers—daring the fates while their *komboloia* ("worry beads") gaily swing from their rear-view mirrors—just drive around for the sheer hell of it. There is only one proven solution to Athens' traffic problems: live television coverage of an important international soccer match. Whenever that happens the streets are deserted.

With the advantage of hindsight, it is easy to see that Athens should have been developed strictly as a cultural and political capital, a kind of Washington D.C. with a pedigree. But its location, so close to the thriving port of Piraeus, always invited commerce; and so it has exploded additionally as the nation's chief centre of industry and trade. Exports of tobacco, wine, oil, figs, marble, bauxite and magnesite pour through the port. More than half of Greece's industrial activity is concentrated in and around the capital: chemical works, soap factories, tanneries, textile mills, flour mills, distilleries, breweries, potteries and carpet factories. Consequently, Athens has no rival in Greece as a place of opportunity and, with average earnings in Athens three times the national average, the city continues to attract rural migrants, even though it has no room to expand except upwards.

Many tourist guide-books still wax lyrical about the unique quality of the brilliant Attic light, about 300 days a year of clear blue skies and crystal waters lapping the beaches on the Saronic Gulf. But guide-books do not deserve all the blame for the shock many visitors feel when they first see the consequences of the city's headlong growth. As Helen Vlachos, Member of Parliament and publisher of the Athens daily newspaper *Kathimerini*, once expressed it: "The visitor, quite justifiably, expects something unique from Athens. He has been misled by history, by legend, by descriptions, by pictures, by a feeling of respect that prevents most people, be they scholars, artists or tourists, from speaking ill of the city that has the honour of surrounding the magnificence of the Acropolis. And yet there it is, an unmistakable fact that no amount of love or sentiment or reverence can hide. Modern Athens is an ugly city, an enormous, sprawling, bone-dry, parkless, treeless, gardenless conglomeration of stone, brick and concrete."

By concentrating on modern developments, it is all too simple to portray Athens as a kind of environmental Armageddon. "Athens needs a major operation," Helen Vlachos has said. "Pollution and traffic must somehow be annihilated. It will have to be done because people have started feeling sick in Athens. Many people say they want to stop smoking, but to stop smoking is nothing. In Athens you have to stop breathing. It is a very, very unhealthy city. And, as it is, I think Athens is a doomed city." Another prominent politician has warned that Athenians could be the first citizens who have to include oxygen masks in their regular attire. Another has blamed air pollution for the falling birth rate: "Some 70 to 75 per cent of young Athenian women show no interest in sexual intercourse because they are living in one of the most intensely polluted cities in the world." (It would be intriguing to know how and by what logic he managed to arrive at that alarming statistic!)

Although the threat from pollution is very real, one needs to bear in mind that Greeks never understate an opinion, least of all a political one. For example, I remember, a few years ago, a mayor of Athens stating: "Our city has lost its charm, calm and local colour, which it preserved until before the Second World War. It has become a sick city, colourless, unsymmetrical, with no personal character." I cannot agree with that statement. Athens may have lost its calm, but it retains an extraordinary abundance of colour and charm—and excitement.

If this were not so, then why are so many visitors moved to return to the city again and again? Are they lured back solely out of that Periclean desire to gaze in wonder on majestic monuments they have already captured on film for their family albums? No, it is much more than that; it is the living city itself—more precisely, the people and their lifestyle— that exerts an almost irresistible magnetic force.

Mexican-born actor Anthony Quinn once explained to me why he had returned to Athens again and again, playing so many Greek roles that many of his fans presumed him to be a Zorba by birth. "It is quite simple," he said. "I think that, without any question, the Greeks are the most wonderful people on earth. They have a natural exuberance uncomplicated by so many of the phoney values of our modern society. They understand how to live with the past and the present. They live in the *now*."

In Athens, this exuberance shines through the grubbiness of modern urban existence. Even though the 19th-Century village has exploded into a traffic-snarled megalopolis, a village atmosphere remains, with every neighbourhood gravitating around its own square or its most popular *kafeneion*—coffee-house—where people congregate every day to eat, drink, talk, and while the hours away. The Athenians live in a concrete jungle; yet, in spirit, they remain close to nature, preserving the communicative pleasures of rural life, brightening up the drabbest cement beehive with flowering plants trained on to trellises to festoon every cornice, ledge and balcony, combating the stench of sulphur dioxide by perfuming the air with the lingering scents of jasmine, basil and lavender.

I doubt whether any European capital has citizens more talkative and gregarious than those of Athens. Certainly, they are the most hospitable of metropolitan breeds. I think it significant that Greek is the only

A fortunate penthouse-dweller, who has created his own green space among the jammed apartment blocks of Athens, pushes an electric mower across the lawn leading to his swimming pool—which itself is awaiting maintenance work in the form of a spring cleaning.

language in which the word for stranger (*xenos*) also means guest; and —in spite of that basically well-founded cliché, "the Greeks had a word for it"—they do not have any equivalent of the English word *stand-offishness*. They will talk to anyone, and about anything and everything. Their curiosity is insatiable; their approach refreshingly open, direct, uninhibited and personal: How much do you earn? What did you pay for that suit? Are you married? How many children do you have?

The Athenians enjoy life to a degree that is totally belied by their end-less political wranglings, their obsessional singing of sad songs, and their driving of cars with kamikaze abandon. More and more, these big-city dwellers are torn between the idealism of the Golden Age and the grey necessities of modern life. Their temperament, says the Greek writer Nicos Demos, fluctuates between exultation and dejection. Yet they retain a passionate love of life—"in the now"—and they do not abuse it. In Athens, one surprisingly finds, suicide and drunkenness are virtually unknown.

All the world has been told of the eternal magic of the Acropolis; the appeal of the modern city is something else. Helen Vlachos has summed it up brilliantly: "After anticipation and then disappointment, there comes a third relationship with Athens. It comes either to people who have stayed a long time in the city or to those who have a special susceptibility to the indefinable Athenian charm and atmosphere. Suddenly you forget the ugliness, throw a veil of invisibility over what is unpleasant, and trip without protest over broken pavements because you now know they are of white marble. You sit at a table of an outdoor café and you begin to discover that Athens is not only a different city, it is a different way of life."

Densely packed apartment blocks spread west of Mount Lycabettus in central Athens. Since 1920, the city has expanded to accommodate a tenfold increase in population, from 300,000 to 3,000,000. But the new buildings have gone up without any over-all development plan or provision for new green spaces.

Physically, Athens is very different from other cities because of its extraordinary lack of historical continuity. Unlike any other great European capital of ancient origin, it has a period of more than 1,500 years—from its sacking by the Goths in the mid-3rd Century A.D. until its rebirth as a capital in 1834—with no buildings of interest to show, aside from a handful of diminutive Byzantine chapels that look like jewel caskets or reliquaries.

Thereafter, any architectural interest focuses on examples of the neoclassical "Othonian" style, and even this period is barely represented on the residential level. During my last visit to Athens, many 19th-Century buildings were falling down or being demolished allegedly in the name of progress. I remember walking down Odos Aristophanes, a street of tanners and shoemakers, and seeing a handsome, two-storey residence in the neoclassical style. Its roof was edged with no fewer than 600 *akroteria*, those decorative tiles in the shape of palmetto leaves that are one of the oldest architectural leitmotifs of Athens. Moreover, the *akroteria* here were graced with heads of Hermes, messenger of Zeus. Yet the building was now a warehouse and marked for demolition.

As I finished counting the *akroteria*, I noticed a workman in blue overalls gazing down at me from the roof. "You want one?" he yelled. "*Neh*," I replied, meaning "yes" (Greek, confusingly, is the only Indo-European language that begins the affirmative with the letter "n").

He leaned over, at what seemed to be risk of life and limb, and disengaged one of the *akroteria* from the cornice. Then, as he moved directly above me, I realized that he aimed to drop this fragile 130-year-old souvenir directly into my hands. Never much of a ball player, I shook my head and retreated across the street. Thereupon, the workman obligingly climbed down from the roof, met me in the middle of Aristophanes Street, and presented me with the beautiful tile.

I reached for my wallet, intending to pay him the $10 that these *akroteria* fetch in the flea market on Pandrossou Street. "*Ochi*," he said; no, he would not take money for a gift. I had an apple in my pocket and so I offered him that. This he accepted with the grace of a king, leaving me with a piece of neoclassical Athens that I still cherish.

Fortunately, some outstanding examples of neoclassical architecture on the grandest scale remain: most notably the University, the National Archaeological Museum, the National Library, and the Academy—a scholarly institution with statues of Apollo and Pallas Athena standing aloft on towering Ionic columns. But otherwise—following the redevelopment boom launched in the 1950s—modern Athens may be described as a jumble of characterless architecture surrounding the most stunning assembly of classical architecture on earth.

At the same time, I cannot agree with those aesthetes who dogmatically label modern Athens an "ugly city" without any qualification. This city— the capital beyond the Acropolis and its surrounds—has at least two redeeming features that would be a major asset to any metropolis. One is the *Ethnikos Kipos*, the National Gardens created in the mid-19th Century immediately south of the old royal palace. In this enchanting oasis of stately palms, shaded walks and leafy ponds, the seemingly impossible becomes possible: peace and solitude only two minutes' walk from the roaring vortex of Syntagma Square.

The other saving grace of modern Athens can be reached eight blocks north-west of the National Gardens, beyond the exclusive residential quarter of Kolonaki. There, the land rises steeply to form nature's *pièce de résistance* in Athens: the conical, fir-clad limestone rock of Lycabettus that rears up in the centre of the city to a dominant 886 feet. Named for the packs of wolves (*lyki*) that roamed over its slopes in classical times, Mount Lycabettus is crowned by the minuscule Byzantine-style chapel of Aghios Georgios (St. George)—a thimble compared with the next highest man-made landmark, the Parthenon, but commanding a far more spectacular view of the capital.

In terms of modern warfare, Lycabettus, not the Acropolis, would be the automatic first choice for creating a city-fortress in the basin of Athens. But those first settlers of 7,000 years ago lacked the weaponry to secure a hill with a gradient of approximately 45 degrees on all sides. For their strategic purposes, the far smaller Acropolis was perfect: sheer on three sides, approachable only from the west; crowned with a gently sloping oval plateau, 1,082 feet long and 557 feet wide at its extremes; and having water readily available from underground springs. So Lycabettus was never fortified and it remains unspoiled, in spite of the additions of a funicular railway (running discreetly below the surface of the south-east flank) and restaurants nestling unobtrusively near the summit.

In its own way, Lycabettus is—or rather should be—as important to Athens as the Acropolis itself. "Sacrilege!" I hear the culture fanatics complaining. But what use is a city that has a spirit and heart of finest Pentelic marble and no lungs with which to breathe? Lycabettus is Athens' citadel of sanity, the eye of the hurricane in which nature reigns supreme. Leaving the serpentine road that girdles this limestone rock, I have rambled for hours in the shade of its pine trees, exploring vaguely defined pathways, hearing not a sound from the city directly below, and encountering no more life than a solitary Kolonaki resident walking his dog or a professional soccer player (the new living gods of Greece) out on a strenuous training run.

If the city of New York had the topography of Athens, I have no doubt at all that Lycabettus would be a kind of high-rise Central Park, a great outdoors within the metropolis to be frequented by lovers of the open-air: joggers, students, painters, courting couples and so on. But this doesn't happen in Athens; Lycabettus never teems with citizens escaping the pollution below—a fact that contributes greatly to its unspoiled charm.

Stucco caryatids on a decaying balcony indicate the neoclassical origins of a building whose ground floor has been converted into shops. The style evolved in western Europe and was brought to Athens by Bavaria-born King Otho after his installation on the Greek throne in 1833. It dominated Athenian architecture until the 1920s—but is now fast disappearing under the onslaught of highrise development.

In Athens' northern suburb of Kiffissia, stone lions guard the grounds of a derelict villa embellished with typical neoclassical features— Doric columns, iron balustrades and pediments above the windows. During the 19th Century, many imposing villas were built in Kiffissia, which is still popular as a summer resort.

This neglect reflects a curious aspect of the character of Athenians. Sensually, they are close to the earth; but they are not especially interested in the pastoral scene *per se*, even though they themselves are cut off from the countryside by mountains and sea. Somehow, these gregarious people feel vulnerable in the open countryside. It produces a kind of *angst*. Out on the open road, I have sometimes seen a passenger in a bus pulling down the blinds—not, as one might imagine, as a shield against the sun but the empty view and the sense of isolation it stirs.

Quite naturally, of course, these city-dwellers will grab every opportunity in summer to escape their concrete pressure-cookers. On Saturday mornings all roads out of Athens teem with the traffic of people heading for beaches and country chalets. But this mass exodus cannot be explained in terms of the cliché "getting away from it all", because they are never trying to get away from people. Such is their in-bred fear of solitude (they call the condition *erimia*, literally meaning "desert") that they congregate in densely packed masses on a beach while vast expanses of sand are left deserted, much to the delight of foreigners eager to escape the madding crowd and preserve their own peace and quiet and privacy. The Greek word for "private" is *idiotikos*. Only an "idiot" frets about his privacy instead of launching himself into the life of the society around him.

This zest for social life has considerable bearing on the present and future of modern Athens. In 1970, the Greek Chamber of Commerce and Technology warned that the capital would have to be abandoned by its residents in 10 years unless radical measures were taken immediately to combat pollution. They were not taken; the city continues to grow.

Athenians may complain about their worsening environment, but they are not to be persuaded to quit the capital by the prophets of doom. Most citizens agree that Athens offers the most exciting social life to be had anywhere and—unless one considers emigration—the greatest opportunities for making money. At the same time, the prime ambition of the Greek peasant is to become a townsman. "Let's go and live in Athens like human beings" is the rather ironic sentiment commonly heard in rural parts. Given this sort of sentiment, it is folly even to suggest that the Athenian environment may eventually become uninhabitable. In the final analysis, a city is people; and Athens may have the most tenacious and resilient people on earth. Perhaps they lack vision—or rather vigour—in adapting their modern capital to 20th-Century needs; but, as the Acropolis testifies, they belong to the oldest continually inhabited city in the Western world, and that is a fact to which one must give due weight.

An Open-air Cornucopia

At a stall off Omonia Square, a jeweller defends his prices against a hard-bargaining customer. The scale on the counter (background) is used to weigh gold.

Athens, blessed with a mild year-round climate, is one of the few Western capitals where much of the retail trading takes place right in the streets. A central, open-air market starts at Omonia Square and runs along Athinas Street for half a mile before terminating near the Agora—the city's ancient marketplace. At shops, stalls or more impromptu premises along this route, Athenians can buy almost anything imaginable, from fine jewellery and old coins to spare car parts or the services of a whitewasher. Vendors, leery of being overlooked in the throng, often advertise in full voice. *"Kalo, kalo!"* crows a pedlar, bragging that his wares are "Good, good!" Energetic and lengthy bargaining adds to the din. What transactions lose in speed, however, they gain in the satisfaction generated as a simple purchase becomes a lively test of gamesmanship.

A salesman presides over sponges taken from nearby waters. Although the export of natural sponges has dropped sharply, demand remains high in Athens.

His brush held high to attract attention, one of the many whitewashers who congregate on Kotzia Square awaits a customer whose house needs freshening up.

A young vendor hawks koulouria—bread rings studded with sesame seeds.

A one-man emporium offers a selection of goods ranging from soap to shirts.

With an entreating gesture, a shoe-seller cajoles a prospective customer.

Stationed in front of straw used as wrapping, a vendor vows his eggs are fresh.

A fruiterer from the countryside displays his wares. Some food-sellers travel from villages 50 miles away.

House-and-garden tools are bundled and stacked in a stall to attract buyers.

At a shop specializing in metalware, pails and buckets glisten in neat rows.

Traditional designs brighten country-style blouses and wool shoulder bags.

New camping equipment contrasts cheerfully with vintage military gear.

Second-hand hardware festoons a shop. In Athens, new cars and appliances are costly, so used goods and spare parts are in brisk demand.

A merchant surveys old tyres that will be given new treads and new uses: those that are too worn for vehicular duty are fashioned into shoe soles or baskets.

2

Radiance of the Golden Age

Appropriately, the past of Athens is discovered by moving towards the city's heart. The path cannot be managed without some sense of confusion. Even the largest streets, as they near the Acropolis, grow contorted and lose themselves. Along the way, modern Athens—the endless reaches of charmless conformity built in the past few decades—breaks apart, and chaos reigns; vestigial columns and arches, shorn of their once-grand purpose, rise among trolley-buses and offices.

To some visitors, the ancient ruins appear pitiful or ridiculous. The playwright George Bernard Shaw ended a tour of the city in 1899 with the exasperated comment: "I am quit of Athens and its stupid classic Acropolis and smashed pillars." But most visitors sense in the ruined heart a portion of the identity of the new city. These worn and fractured relics certify Athens as the focal point of a glorious civilization. To live in their presence is to share, no matter how tenuously, one of the great passages of human history.

As early as 5000 B.C., the limestone plateau of the Acropolis was the home of a Neolithic people who spoke an unknown language. The very name Athens was perhaps theirs—it is not Greek—and they left their memory on the plateau in the physical form of fractured earthenware and figures of a fertility goddess with nubile hips and spiky breasts. From such early times, perhaps, developed the worship of the dust-coloured snakes and small owls that haunted the Acropolis—a worship that continued until well into the first millennium B.C., when the owl became the symbol of the goddess Athena.

These earliest Athenians were farmers and herdsmen who lived in huts and wove a simple cloth. But probably by 1900 B.C. the first Greek-speaking invaders had arrived from the north—pastoral warriors whose conquests were followed by an age of darkness. The ancient Greeks, including the Athenians, were an amalgam of such invading waves of Indo-Europeans with the more settled peoples that preceded them. In some areas, the invasions continued to stir havoc until the 12th Century B.C. But in Athens, the destruction subsided as early as 1600 B.C. Shadowy rulers—half-man, half-myth—appear during this period, among them the serpent-bodied Cecrops and Erechtheus, and the hero Theseus, whose military exploits have perhaps come down to us in the legend of how he slew the Minotaur in its labyrinth in Crete.

By the 13th Century B.C., the Acropolis emerged as a feudal stronghold, with gates and walls on the summit. Caves in its slopes served as places

A marble bust now residing at the Vatican Museum in Rome evokes the cool authority of Pericles, the statesman-general who dominated Athens from 461 to 429 B.C. At his urging—and in spite of bitter opposition on the grounds of expense—the Parthenon and other magnificent temples were constructed on the Acropolis to replace shrines that had been burnt to the ground by invading Persians in 480 B.C.

of worship. Down a cleft in the rock's heart, the Athenians cut a series of stairways that plunged 120 feet to a natural well. Above the rock footings there were timber steps, but they rotted away long ago. In any case, it was probably this clammy fissure and its life-giving sliver of water that preserved the citadel against the last wave of besieging Greek invaders from the north—brown-haired Dorians with iron weapons in their hands, who extended their rule over all the rest of Greece in the 12th Century B.C.

Even as late as the 10th Century B.C., it is said, the Dorians made a last attempt to capture Athens. An oracle had promised them victory provided they spared the city's king. But Codrus, the ruler of Athens, heard of this prophecy, entered the enemy camp in the guise of a peasant and deliberately provoked its soldiers into killing him. The Dorians lost heart, and the city was never taken; its people thus remained of a very subtle and mixed Greek strain (they called themselves Ionians) that was to bear brilliant fruit in centuries to come. It is said, too, that from this time dates the end of Athens' monarchy, since no man was deemed worthy to follow Codrus as king. Instead, the city was thereafter ruled by magistrates—at first appointed for life, but later elected annually. It was the slow dawn of democracy.

Through the centuries following the death of Codrus, a new balance of political power developed in Athens. In spite of agrarian troubles, Athens grew rich by her silver mines and enterprising overseas trade, and soon a wealthy bourgeoisie began to challenge the dominance of the old feudal aristocracy. By the early 6th Century B.C., Athens and other cities produced bodies of heavily armed citizen-soldiers, called hoplites. Membership of these phalanxes, which became the backbone of Athenian military strength, was open to any citizen who could afford to buy his own armour; the result was the formation of a democratic soldiery whose existence struck a bitter blow at the warrior nobility.

In spite of advances in their form of government, the Athenians of these times left only a faint impress on the Acropolis. Today, their cave sanctuaries and the rough-hewn walls they built, reassembled by archaeologists, go almost unnoticed next to the beauties of a later age. Whenever I ascend the Acropolis, I am struck by the cultural divide between the crudeness of the city's earliest times and the refined brilliance of its classical era. How did such a transformation occur? What happened in those centuries between Codrus, the last king, and Pericles, the supreme statesman who led Athens, when still a city of a mere 250,000, to its apogee of glory in the 5th Century B.C.?

No one, I think, has quite explained this miracle. Tradition holds that Athens became the refuge of civilized men who came from all over Greece, fleeing the scourge of the Dorians. Later, a self-made merchant class arose, and economic and agrarian reform brought greater affluence. But the miracle is not that of Athens alone—nor even of Greece alone.

As far back as the 12th Century B.C., foreign invasion and the pressures of over-population had caused a host of adventurers to leave their homes in Greece and establish numerous colonies around the Aegean and along the shores of the eastern Mediterranean. And in these places, as well as in the mother country, some alchemy of blood and circumstance produced a new vision of the world.

An early glimmer was recorded six centuries before Christ, in the Greek city of Miletus on the coast of Asia Minor. Here, according to Aristotle, a merchant and philosopher named Thales asked himself, "What are all things made of?"—and himself answered, "Water." The question, of course, was more remarkable than the answer. It foreshadowed the classical Greek desire to find the simple and essential in the world's multiplicity. Before Thales, many Middle Eastern cultures—especially the Egyptian and Sumerian—had developed science from observation, but they never reached for abstract cosmological principles beyond their mass of facts. Facts, to them, were controlled by the Divine; the Divine was the measure of all things. With Thales—who saw water where other men saw God—reason ousted faith.

This spirit of inquiry and self-confidence belonged peculiarly to the Greeks. In politics, of course, it could lead to deep unrest. For a century after 650 B.C., Athens was shaken by a series of internal revolutions, led by wealthy citizens eager to match their newly acquired affluence with political power. But, in the year 507 B.C., the Athenians finally established a full-fledged democracy, in which religion and civic pride were centred on the goddess Athena, symbol and protectress of the city. This faith and pride can still be sensed today, vibrant in the beautiful frieze that once encircled the Parthenon, the greatest of Athens' temples on the Acropolis. The marble reliefs of the frieze—now mostly in the British Museum— portray the great Panathenaic processions that were staged in the city every fourth year to celebrate the birth of the goddess. Along a route that led through the old marketplace at the foot of the Acropolis, the procession carried a new robe for Athena's wooden statue that stood on the plateau above, and heifers and rams were led to sacrifice at her altar.

In the friezes, placidly seated gods look on as the people of the city move in ordered groups—not so much individuals as a solemn flow of beautiful robes and perfected faces. The stately men and women carrying pitchers and instruments of sacrifice, the quietly conversing citizens, even the animals are lit by the sculptor with the radiance of their ceremony. A group of young aristocrats covers the distance on horseback. Those at the rear restrain their mounts, whose bunched legs and curved-in necks give a sense of unbearably controlled energy. But farther along the frieze the pace of the horses quickens, the manes flare out, and the hoofs strike free, until they are released into a glorious canter. In front of the horsemen go chariots, each holding a heavily armed warrior whose globular helmet

Viewed from Philopappos Hill, the temples on the Acropolis still dominate Athens, old and new. Beyond, on the right, is the conical hill of Mount Lycabettus.

haloes him in a fan-like plume. And in front of these the procession again seems to slow, held back by the solemn tread of magistrates and priests, and the heavy march of sacrificial beasts. The sculptor has conceived the procession as more than mere ritual; it is a hymn of praise to the gods and to the city, each inseparable from the other.

In 490 B.C., the new civic spirit was put to the test. A swollen Persian empire, straddling half the eastern Mediterranean, sent an expeditionary force to punish Athens for supporting a revolt of the Greek cities of Asia Minor. The invaders landed at Marathon, on the coast of Attica, and there, in a heady moment of history, were hurled back by 9,000 Athenians and their allies. But 10 years later, the Persian king Xerxes sent a colossal army of perhaps 200,000 men marching overland into northern Greece, whose cities went down before it. In Athens, the People's Assembly was divided over what to do. Its most far-sighted politician, Themistocles, wanted to stem the advance at the narrow pass of Thermopylae in the north; he further recommended that, if the Persians could not be stopped there, the populace of Athens should be evacuated to the Aegean island of Salamis by means of the city-state's newly built naval fleet. Others wanted to defend their homes at all costs. The issue was presented to the revered oracle of Delphi, which—in the enigmatic way of oracles—pronounced that "only the wooden wall will not fail". Themistocles interpreted this wall to be the fleet, but his opponents declared it to be the wooden palisade that circled the Acropolis. Meanwhile, Xerxes was marching southwards unopposed.

Eventually, Themistocles won the debate in the Assembly. Fortunately for the Athenians, the task of fighting at Thermopylae was assumed by their allies; 1,500 men, with a nucleus of 300 from Sparta, died there in a valiant but vain attempt to hold the precipitous pass against the Persian horde. As the main Greek force fell back towards the Peloponnese, Themistocles organized the retreat to Salamis, leaving behind a token force to defend the Acropolis. From its heights this doomed contingent watched the Saronic Gulf fill with Athenian transports as their compatriots fled across the sea; a day later the vanguard of the Persian army arrived and their ships came nosing up the coast.

Perhaps at the behest of Themistocles, the wooden statue of Athena, the most sacred totem of all, had been evacuated to Salamis with the populace. The goddess herself, it seemed, was abandoning the city. For some days the defenders held out, rolling stones and fragments of the Acropolis' columns on to their assailants. But the Persians discovered a narrow stairway leading upwards from a cave-sanctuary on the northern slope of the Acropolis, and by this ancient and perilous ascent, they finally gained a foothold on the plateau. The defenders' spirit broke. Some committed suicide by hurling themselves from the walls. The rest took refuge in the Temple of Athena—the ancestor of the Parthenon—from which they

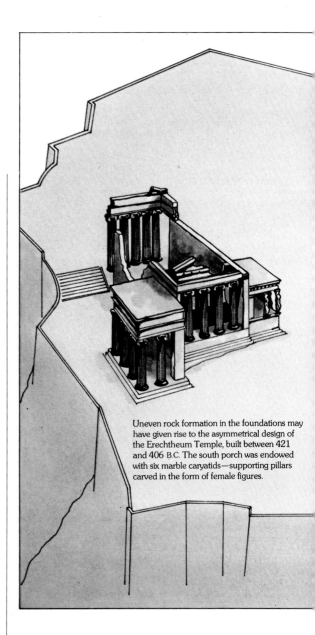

Uneven rock formation in the foundations may have given rise to the asymmetrical design of the Erechtheum Temple, built between 421 and 406 B.C. The south porch was endowed with six marble caryatids—supporting pillars carved in the form of female figures.

Acropolis Masterworks

The four buildings erected on the Acropolis in the 5th Century B.C. marked the zenith of classical architecture. The Parthenon, built first, used the severe Doric order—bulky columns with plain rectangular capitals—to achieve a triumphant grandeur that is undiminished by the temple's present ruined state. The next projects were the Propylaea gateway, also largely Doric in style, and the little Temple of Athena Nike, which employed the lighter Ionic order—slender columns capped by delicate scrolls. Finally, the Ionic style reached perfection in the crisply carved capitals and friezes of the Erechtheum.

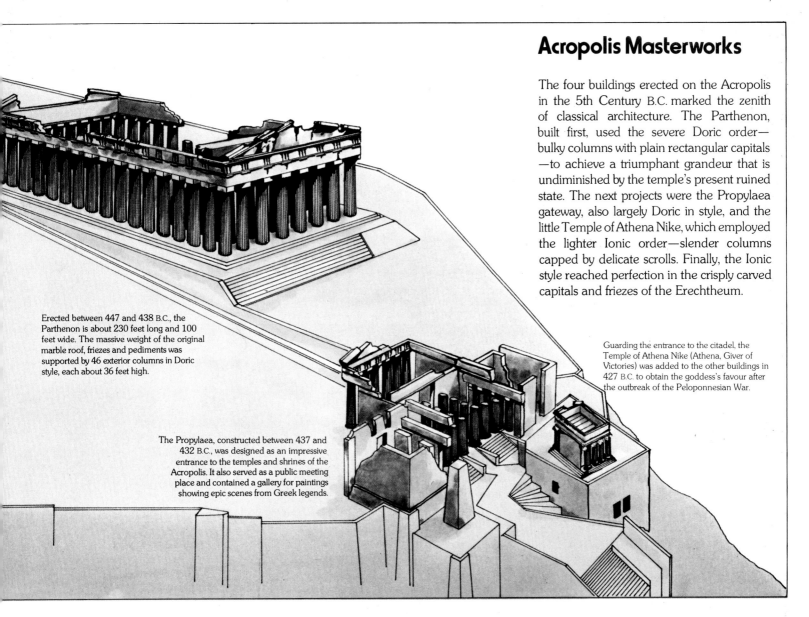

Erected between 447 and 438 B.C., the Parthenon is about 230 feet long and 100 feet wide. The massive weight of the original marble roof, friezes and pediments was supported by 46 exterior columns in Doric style, each about 36 feet high.

The Propylaea, constructed between 437 and 432 B.C., was designed as an impressive entrance to the temples and shrines of the Acropolis. It also served as a public meeting place and contained a gallery for paintings showing epic scenes from Greek legends.

Guarding the entrance to the citadel, the Temple of Athena Nike (Athena, Giver of Victories) was added to the other buildings in 427 B.C. to obtain the goddess's favour after the outbreak of the Peloponnesian War.

were dragged and butchered. Then the Persians sacked the shrines—temples to divinities and the early kings—and set them on fire. Even today, where the Parthenon stands rocked on these earlier stones, you may see the indelible marks of those flames.

The Athenians did not wait long to avenge themselves. Themistocles lured the Persian fleet into the narrows of Salamis and there demolished it with his heavy galleys. The next summer, in a battle near the town of Plataea, the last of the Persian army was driven from the land. It was an astonishing victory. There were still men living in Athens who could remember 70 years before when the city had been little more than a minor local power, threatened by anarchy.

For the next three decades, the people devoted themselves to rebuilding their shattered city in a new and grander image. An enormous perimeter wall, government offices, colonnades, public squares—a whole secular metropolis arose north-west of the Acropolis. If you stand today among the ruins of the ancient Agora—the city's public meeting-place—you may still decipher traces of that early splendour. To the south, the nearby hill of the Areopagus, seat of Athens' rulers in pre-democratic days, rises above the Pnyx, the hill of the People's Assembly. To the west, stands the Temple of the fire-god Hephaestus—the most perfectly preserved of Greek shrines, whose outer columns and inner sanctuary are almost complete. And all

Destined to be put in a museum and replaced by glass fibre copies, the decaying caryatids of the Erechtheum Temple on the Acropolis await removal beneath a makeshift roof that keeps off pollution-tainted rain. Moulds of the original statue-pillars were made in the 19th Century, permitting the creation of faithful copies.

about, in a half-decipherable scribbling of stones over the ground, lie the altars, council chambers and porticos of the Golden Age.

Yet for more than 30 years after the Persian sack, the shrines on the Acropolis itself remained in ruins. Before the battle of Plataea, Athenian soldiers had taken this group oath: "I will not rebuild any of the temples that have been burned and destroyed by the barbarians, but I will let them be left as a memorial, to those who come after, of the sacrilege of the barbarians." Only in 449 B.C. after peace was made with Persia, did the Athenians feel absolved from their oath. By now Athens, with a powerful navy manned by the poorest and toughest of the men, headed a defence league whose members included almost all the Greek cities of the Aegean. The city's population, its trade, its industries had all expanded. In knowledge and in art the tentative dawn had passed into a dazzling morning. And within a few generations this little city-state—no larger than a small industrial town in Europe or America—had produced more men of genius than had half the empires of the East together.

As early as 461 B.C., the Assembly was dominated by the remarkable statesman Pericles, who envisaged the Acropolis crowned with architectural splendours—principally a handsome gateway leading to an enormous temple—to which the eyes of all Greece would turn in pride. To finance these projects he proposed to empty the defence league's treasury —a plan that at once drew a hurricane of abuse from conservatives in the Assembly. "The Greeks must be outraged," their spokesman stormed. "They must consider this an act of barefaced tyranny, when they see that with their own contributions, extorted from them by force for the war against the Persians, we are gilding our city, which, for all the world like a wanton woman, adds to her wardrobe precious stones. . . ."

Pericles was not motivated by piety. He appears rather to have been a freethinker who believed in harnessing religion to the State. The Parthenon itself, centrepiece of his plan, would be a monument less to a goddess than to a people—a memorial of victory over the Persians, and of the light of reason over a barbarian darkness. And it seems that the Assembly, in which every free Athenian had the right to vote, granted Pericles a majority less in the fervour of religion than in expectation of a job—for such a project would employ thousands, from masons and carpenters to clerks and muleteers.

When I re-explored the Acropolis recently, another army numbering thousands was present. As I toiled up the broad stairs towards the summit, a great throng of tourists laden with cameras and guide-books walked behind and in front of me. A sledgehammer sun beat down, reflecting off rock and stone; but in spite of crowds and the heat of the day, a sense of wonder and elation mounted within me as I neared the top. To my right stood the little temple of Athena Nike—meaning "the Victorious"—built

Centuries of Splendour and Decay

B.C. c. 5000	Neolithic peoples settle on and around the Acropolis, a limestone hill with a commanding view of the Attic plain
c. 2000	First Hellenes invade Greece from the north. The Hellenic people, known as Ionians, settle in Attica
1200-1100	Refugees from areas invaded by the Dorian marauders from northern Greece, flock into Athens and surrounding countryside. Many migrate to Aegean Islands; others found Greek colonies on west coast of Asia Minor, ultimately called Ionia
c. 900-800	Rise of Greek city-states. Townships of Attica federate under leadership of Athens
507	New Athenian constitution grants equal political rights to all citizens
500-494	Aided by Athens, Ionian Greeks stage unsuccessful revolt against Persian rule
490	Darius of Persia launches attack on mainland Greece, starting the Persian wars. Persians repelled by Athenian army at battle of Marathon
483	Themistocles, archon of Athens, builds powerful fleet
481	Greek states, under Sparta's leadership, meet to plan a united effort against the Persians
480	King Xerxes, son of Darius, renews Persian offensive against Greece, defeating Spartans at Thermopylae. Athens evacuated before Persians sack the city. Athenian fleet restores Greek fortunes with crushing naval victory in Straits of Salamis
479	Last major battles of the war, at Plataea and Mycale, end in defeat for Persia. Growth of Athens as a maritime power rivalling Sparta
478-476	Athens organizes Delian League, a maritime alliance of Greek states, including Ionia, to counter threat of Persian reprisals
461	Pericles becomes most influential Athenian politician. His policy of imperial expansion leads to increasing friction with Sparta
459-446	Intermittent warfare between Athens and Sparta ends in declaration of Thirty Years' Peace
457	Defensive long walls built between Athens and Piraeus
454-453	Treasury of the Delian League transferred from Delos to Athens. Subsequently, the funds were used by Pericles to finance lavish programme of public building
447-431	Work begins on the Parthenon, ushering in the so-called Golden Age of Athens. City's inhabitants include the philosopher Socrates, the historian Herodotus, the poet Pindar and the dramatists Sophocles and Euripides
431-404	Peloponnesian War between Athens and Sparta
429	Pericles dies of plague
404	Athens surrenders to Sparta
387	Plato founds his Academy in Athens
338	King Philip II of Macedonia defeats Athens and its allies at battle of Chaeronia and assumes leadership of Greece
335	Aristotle establishes Peripatetic School of Philosophy at Athens
197-148	Rome, now in its ascendancy, sends legions to crush the power of Macedonia and eventually puts all of Greece under a Roman governor
88-86	Athens supports rebellion in Asia Minor against Rome. Roman general, Sulla, storms the city, destroying its walls and massacring many of its citizens
27	Emperor Augustus completes construction of Roman Agora in Athens. City acclaimed as centre of learning
A.D. 49	St. Paul preaches to the Athenians
120-128	Emperor Hadrian lives in Athens, endowing the city with a library, gymnasium, pantheon and triumphal arch. Completes Temple of Olympian Zeus, which had been started and abandoned six centuries earlier

to honour the city's protectress. Although an image of Athena with wings was the conventional symbol of victory, the goddess was portrayed wingless in this case; it is said that this was intended to prevent her from taking flight from the city. In fact, the statue disappeared at some unknown point in Athenian history, but the columns and friezes are still intact around her temple.

In front of me, more imposing, the Propylaea gateway gave access to the summit of the Acropolis. This ruined entranceway was a triumph as great, in its way, as that of the Parthenon. It straddled a compressed, uneven site with a monumental span of deep porches and hipped roofs. The outer pillars, like those of the Parthenon, are of the plain, dignified order called Doric. But inside, where they flank the ascending way, they turn to the Ionic style, whose capitals curl into graceful roundels.

For all its grandeur, the Propylaea was conceived primarily as the frame and the herald of a greater endeavour: the Parthenon. Perhaps no other building on earth so epitomizes a culture, or captures with such ghostly accuracy a fleeting moment of time. To many, the Parthenon is not only the sum of a civilization, but the emblem of civilization itself—the victory of order over chaos. That this emblematic role was its builders' intention is made clear in some of the carvings adorning it—depictions of the mythic conquest of the Amazons by the Greeks, the battle between Greeks and Centaurs, the overthrow of the giants by the Olympian gods. To the Athenians, all these legendary encounters signified the triumph of reason over savagery and darkness.

The labour of creating this immortal structure was immense. Twenty-two thousand tons of marble were quarried and hauled on sleds down the slopes of Mount Pentelicon 10 miles away, then reloaded into wagons or giant wooden frames that were hauled by as many as 30 oxen along a reinforced road to the foot of the Acropolis, and from there winched and dragged up the citadel's slope. This preliminary work, and the perfecting of the temple platform, took three years.

The Parthenon—which means "the shrine of the virgin"—was built partly on the site of its ruined predecessor, but far transcended it in magnificence and subtlety. Larger than any previous Greek temple, it was hedged with 46 columns set unusually high and close together. Columns, steps, architraves, pediments, tiles—all were of the white Pentelic marble, glowing fine-grained yet soft enough for precise carving. As seen from the Propylaea, the great temple must have risen beyond the intervening terraces and statues in awesome remoteness and majesty.

On its pediments, the sculptured gods and goddesses crowded into their appointed places and enacted moments of divine drama—the birth of Athena, and her conflict with the sea-god Poseidon for mastery of the city. In ancient times, a worshipper, mounting the temple steps and entering through great doors that were panelled in bronze and ivory, would have

Introducing a note of modernity among the decorous figures of classical Athens, a footsore sightseer changes her socks in the Theatre of Dionysus.

plunged from harsh sunlight into sudden dusk. And there, almost 40 feet high, the goddess Athena gazed down on him. Robed in solid gold, her expression one of frigid and immortal power, she held the rim of her shield with one hand and extended the other to support a small winged effigy of herself. Her helmet, crowned with griffins and topped by a sphinx, sent a cascade of plumes behind her back.

The creator of this towering statue, and the mastermind behind the whole inspired readornment of the Acropolis, was the great sculptor Phidias, in collaboration with Pericles himself. No expense was spared. Although the statue's core was wood, the flesh was ivory, the eyes were gems, and the robe contained more than 2,500 pounds of gold (the cost of the robe alone far exceeded that of the rest of the Parthenon). In the 3rd Century B.C., the overlay of gold was removed to pay the merchants of the ruling tyrant of the day; at some later point, the derobed effigy was destroyed—possibly by fire.

The ultimate fate of the Parthenon itself was little happier. In the 6th Century A.D., the sanctuary was transformed into a Christian church and its dedication passed from the warrior-virgin Athena to the Blessed Virgin Mary. Nine hundred years after that, the conquering Turks turned it into a mosque and girt it with a minaret. Then, in 1687, Venetian forces that had already subdued much of Greece laid siege to Athens. The Turks took refuge on the Acropolis, using the Parthenon as a powder magazine. On September 26, the commander of the Venetians, a Swedish mercenary field marshal who claimed to love the classics, ordered his guns to fire on the temple. A shell dropped through the roof and the building was instantly blown in two. The shrine walls burst, 28 columns collapsed and the roof was blown to bits. After the Turks surrendered, the classics-loving field marshal tried to take away the sculptured horses from the west pediment; but as they were being lowered, the tackle broke and they were smashed to pieces.

Early in the 19th Century, the equally acquisitive but more careful Lord Elgin, British Ambassador to Turkey, acquired permission to carry away much of the temple's choicest sculpture; the relics ended up in the British Museum. Thereafter, the site became a picking-ground for amateur antiquaries and gentlefolk making the Grand Tour. Only after Greece won independence in 1833 did archaeologists pluck away the detritus of foreign centuries and, piece by piece, restore almost all the fallen columns.

Now, from the shadow of the Propylaea, where tourists were huddling out of the sun's glare, I looked across at a building that Phidias would barely recognize. A pale skeleton, beautiful and stricken, the Parthenon leaks the sun and sky at every point. Its columns are wasted and torn, its pediments cracked, its sanctuary in ruins.

It is forbidden so much as to breathe on a stone of it. Guards whistle at the first intimate approach to it. But as I walked around its nakedness, the

With the aid of his transistor radio, a guard whiles away the hours in the Temple of Hephaestus, overlooking the Greek Agora. The well-preserved building is known as the Theseum because many of its exterior statues depict the adventures of Theseus, the legendary king of Athens who slew the Cretan Minotaur.

refinement of its body grew on me. If any building is a symbol of mathematical precision, it is surely this one. Yet, in the entire temple there is scarcely a straight line. The Greeks realized that straight lines in architecture can create clumsy optical illusions: vertical lines bend, horizontals sag. To compensate for such tricks of the eye, the whole base of the Parthenon façade lifts gradually at the centres of all four sides, and each column, by a subtlety called *entasis*, swells in the middle before narrowing again at the top. This, and the ever-so faint leaning inwards of every column, enhances the impression of soaring height. (It has been calculated that if the axes of all the apparently vertical columns were extended upwards, they would eventually meet almost a mile above the Parthenon.)

Nonetheless, as I circled this frail geometry I realized that I was walking in a dream, concocted by romantics. The original Parthenon was vivid—garish, even—with colour. Once, all the statues, friezes, and reliefs were daubed in heavy black, red, and blue tints. The sculptured gods moved in a swirl of gilt and ochre. Their eyes glittered with cut glass; their hands clutched bronze swords or tridents, long since gone. Even architectural features were picked out brightly: extravagantly gilded ceilings, exuberant mouldings, and sprouting, black-painted finials. Now, even the bare stone looks different; the iron particles in the marble have oxidized over the centuries, maturing its whiteness to pale gold.

Vividness was natural to the ancient Greeks. Many 19th-Century romantics may have imagined them as creatures of abstract nobility, but the truth was more human and more various. The romantics were—and still are—mortified to find the modern Greek so different, both physically and temperamentally, from their conception of his ancestor. They conclude that the ancient race was subsumed during Slavic, Albanian and Turkish invasions. And so, in part, it was.

But the ancient Greeks who strove for balance and harmony were a passionate people seeking what they rarely actually had. The ancient Athenians, like their descendants of today, were ambitious and gregarious. To watch a group of modern Greeks is to witness a race of natural orators and politicians—mercurial, anarchic, intelligent. And so it was in Pericles' day. The Parthenon itself was raised in the midst of bitter lobbying and in-fighting, as well as accusations of embezzlement (Phidias, a target for the charges, had to flee the city). It was a monument to the vigorous—and enduring—Athenian personality.

The Golden Age was pitifully shortlived. Pericles died of plague in the year 429 B.C., and a quarter of the citizens perished with him. In the long, ruinous conflict called the Peloponnesian War, between 431 and 404 B.C., the Athenian empire fought Sparta and its allies, and eventually lost.

During this time, the last temple was built on the Acropolis—a graceful, irregular building named the Erechtheum. It enshrined a congeries of relics that had been sacred to the Athenians for centuries: a spring

The Tower of the Winds (right) dominates the Roman Agora, the market begun more than a century after Greece came under the sway of Rome in 146 B.C.

where the god Poseidon supposedly left his mark, the tomb of the serpent-king Cecrops, an olive-wood statue of Athena, a holy snake that was fed on honeycakes, and other divine items. Perhaps it is not chance that in the hard days of the war men turned from the rational splendour of Athena's Parthenon to honour these older and darker powers—the protectors of their fathers—and met their multiple claims by erecting an Ionic building of eccentric beauty.

Against the masculine symmetry of the Parthenon 50 yards away, the Erechtheum opposes a feminine charm. Its slim, deeply fluted columns lend it a harmony all its own. Its details are lavish and delicate. Sculptured maidens—named "caryatids" after the handsome women of Karyai on the Peloponnese peninsula—hold up the southern porch in lieu of pillars. Their stone faces have been eroded almost beyond recognition by the effects of air-pollution.

Pollution threatens the entire Acropolis. Its buildings have suffered more erosion in the last 40 years than in the previous 24 centuries. The chief villain is the sulphur dioxide poured into the air by heavy industry, car exhaust fumes and domestic central heating. This gas combines with moisture to form a deadly acid that turns the surface of marble into a gypsum so powdery that rain or the mere touch of a hand can scatter it.

Nor is that all. Early in this century, steel pins and girders were inserted in the joints of the buildings to secure them. The ancient Greeks had done the same—but they took the precaution of coating their iron joints with lead, which rendered them almost rustproof. The originals have stood the test of centuries; however, the modern pins, oxidized, are now expanding and cracking the marble.

Lastly, the feet of many millions of tourists have worn away the surface of rock and pavement, threatening to obliterate humbler features that sometimes go unnoticed: frail foundations, sockets for the base of vanished statues, the direction of ancient paths.

By the mid-1970s it had become clear that the wonders of the Acropolis could be saved only by drastic measures. A group of Swiss engineers, thinking big, proposed that the entire summit, with all its temples, be enclosed in a glass bubble—a grotesque scheme that was quickly rejected by the Athens government. Instead, the government resolved to remove the endangered sculptures of the Parthenon, replace them with glass fibre copies and house the originals in a new museum. The city also embarked on a project to replace the steel reinforcements with new versions made of almost invulnerable titanium—a huge and delicate task of dismantling and reassembling that will take many years.

The treasures of the Acropolis represent just a fraction of the classical legacies threatened by Athens' polluted air. Leaning over the south wall of the great citadel, I looked towards the sea into an impenetrable haze. A hundred feet below me, empty and secretive, the Theatre of

Dionysus lay cupped in its slope. The broken seats, fanned in a horseshoe of grey stone, once held 15,000 spectators. Many tiers have disintegrated and lie in rubble circled by cypress and pine trees, but those closest to the front—the seats of Dionysus' priests—retain their curved stone backs and shed a ghostly intimacy over the stage. Although built under uncertain circumstances a hundred years after the Golden Age, this sad and beautiful theatre occupies the same site as another, where a century earlier the masters of Athenian drama—Aeschylus, Sophocles, Euripides, Aristophanes—brought a new art to flower.

Both tragedy and comedy had their origins in the Greek worship of Dionysus, god of wine and fertility. Tragedy sprang from the singing and acting of the ancient myth of his death and resurrection; comedy derived from a ribald and drunken procession celebrating his divine powers. Out of such beginnings the Athenian playwrights moved, in a single century, from the austere tragedies of Aeschylus to the mockery of Aristophanes, to whom nothing was sacred; from Sophocles' human grandeur to the near-agnosticism of Euripides. The old art of performing these plays, involving masked actors and a ritual chorus, is lost. But the Greek National Theatre, which stages drama every summer in the nearby Roman Odeon of Herodes Atticus, has resurrected them in its own inspired way, deploying its chorus in rhythmic incantation and stylized dance. Thus, something of that ancient majesty is savoured still by Athenians and tourists near the place where Western theatre was born.

On the opposite side of the Acropolis, other ruins from the classical age abound. Descending from the citadel and walking northwards along the broken spine of the Panathenaic Way, I entered the Agora, the meeting-place of ancient Athens. Here, only the long, two-storeyed colonnade called the Stoa of Attalus—meticulously reconstructed in the 1950s by American archaeologists—gives any sense of a living past. Here too, among the modest ruins of its history, one realizes what a little place this great city was—nowhere exceeding a mile in breadth.

If the Acropolis was the heart of the city, the Agora was its voice. Not only was this meeting-place the centre of commerce, but of much teaching and government as well. Together with the Assembly, it lay at the core of the *polis*—that peculiarly Greek concept that is translated "city-state", but which more specifically means a body of men sharing common ideals. As a system of government, the *polis* was viable only for a small and free community like Athens. It resembled, in essence, an enormous family, fostering all of its members' activities and demanding their service. It was both the audience and judge of their actions—a stimulus to excellence and to the pursuit of honour. "The city," wrote the lyric poet Simonides, "is the teacher of the man."

Yet, more than half of all Athenians—women and slaves—had no vote at all. Among Greek city-states, Athens seems to have treated its women

A Legendary Motif

For more than 2,000 years, the wild acanthus plant that thrives in the dry soil of Greece has been a favourite decorative motif of Athenian artists and architects. The most celebrated depiction of the plant is the capital of the Corinthian column—shown above, with a real acanthus growing in the foreground; according to legend, the Athenian sculptor Callimachus created this design in the 5th Century B.C. after seeing some acanthus leaves curling gracefully around a basket that had been left on the grave of a Corinthian girl.

A modern version of the capital adorns a column framing the entrance of a new Byzantine-style church in central Athens (middle row, second right). Some of the other acanthus motifs gathered here are more stylized, such as the fan-shaped leaf radiating from a pediment above Athens University (top row, second left), or the clean-lined decorative element for a modern office building (bottom row, second from right). In the middle row, at centre, the painted side of a chest displays an extra ingredient—spikes of flowers that the acanthus plant puts forth once a year.

worse than many. No doubt, as today, women were vociferous in the home. But they were excluded from public life and, because the ideal of the time was masculine and "heroic", expressing itself less in tenderness than in energy, a man might naturally seek his fulfilment with other men, even in love. The woman, meanwhile, bore him his children and controlled his house—a simple home in every case, for frugality was the rule far into the 4th Century B.C. Rooms rising in two storeys about a courtyard, a few select pieces of furniture and ceramics—this was the limit even of a rich man's ostentation.

As for slaves, it has been estimated that there was about one for every two citizens. More than half of these were domestics and—in contrast to the city's women—they were better treated than in most of Greece. Certainly they were legally protected. Only the 10,000 slaves in the silver mines near the coast suffered the usual lot of serfs; economic necessity seems here to have overruled conscience.

But no specific shortcomings can blind us to the Athenians' overall accomplishments. In an age of mass bigotry and servitude, they inaugurated a life in which intellectual inquiry ousted blind faith in magic, in which men had the courage to live not for a tyrant god or a god king but for the honour and wholeness of man himself.

Nowhere is this clearer than in their way of death. North-west of the Agora stretch the burial-grounds of the Ceramicus, the potters' quarter where Athens laid its heroes to rest. The ashes of Pericles himself were interred here, and those of Athenians who fell in war. Some of the funerary monuments have been preserved where they stood, many others are housed in museums; but in all of them—sarcophagi, tablets, tiny chapels—the same message is clear. They are celebrations of the glory of life, not pleas for a future after it. The Greeks looked with courage into the darkness of death and saw nothing hopeful there. Death, to most of them, was merely a shadow of the living light, and the dead were no more than gibbering ghosts in fields of asphodel. In Homer's *Odyssey*, the shade of Achilles himself declares that he would rather be a labourer on earth than king over all the dead.

So their funerary stones are not carved with pious expectations; instead, they commemorate the individual, seen as he was when alive and at his best. The muscled warrior stares ahead, proud and ready for battle; a little girl fondles her pigeons; and an old woman, surrounded by her family, bids them farewell with a serene inclination of her head and a restrained touching of hands. In death, the Greek could be consoled only if his glory was perpetuated in men's memory. So the poet Simonides celebrated the memory of the Spartans fallen at Plataea, whose "valour lifts them yet into the splendour from the night beneath".

But by the end of the Peloponnesian War, this heroic outlook had already dimmed. After a winter siege, the Spartans occupied the city in

VEDUTA DEL CAST: D ACROPOLIS DALLA PARTE DI TRAMONTANA

The Parthenon, used as a powder magazine during a Venetian siege of Athens in 1687, splits apart in a violent explosion set off by a well-aimed shell. The blast failed to destroy both a mosque built within the temple and the minaret seen standing beside it in this contemporary view of the disaster: they were finally demolished after Greece won independence in the 19th Century.

404 B.C. and pulled down fortifications built by Themistocles. Although they withdrew a year later, leaving behind an unsteady democracy, Athens was no longer united. Something vital had died. The city's people were so unsure of themselves that in 399 B.C. they tried and condemned to death the great philosopher Socrates for undermining the state by his endless public questionings. Democracy was on the defensive. Both Socrates and his disciple Plato, whose Academy of Philosophy decorates this later period with a new distinction, looked to a more authoritarian ideal of government.

It was inevitable, perhaps, that the Athenian *polis* should wane. The bold clarity of its ideals was darkened forever by failure in the Peloponnesian War—and, more subtly, by the turning of its people's energies to individual ends. The new age brought luxury and social division. In the army, mercenaries began to take the place of the citizen-soldier. In the temple, faith drew closer to mysticism. As for philosophy, Aristotle, the pupil of Plato, was more practical and less visionary than his master; in 335 B.C., he founded the famous Peripatetic School, which stressed empirical science rather than abstract reasoning. Two other important schools of thought also grew up during the period—Cynicism and Stoicism. But in contrast to the life-embracing attitudes of the 5th Century, both schools were austerely moral and defensive, even ascetic.

By the middle of the 4th Century B.C., the populace had already become so self-engrossed that not even Demosthenes, greatest of orators, could rouse it against a new peril from the north. This was Macedonia, once a crude backwater, now a wealthy and belligerent Greek state under the ruthless Philip II. In 338 B.C., Athens and Thebes belatedly combined against the Macedonian threat, but were defeated at the battle of Chaeronea, which has been called the graveyard of the free *polis*. So Athens became a virtual satellite of the growing Macedonian empire.

Two years later, Philip was assassinated and his son Alexander succeeded him. Within 13 years, in 323 B.C., Alexander the Great himself died after conquering the entire Persian empire, and at once his dominions were divided between his Macedonian generals. Athens revolted once more against Macedonia, but was again defeated. This time the blow was mortal. For decades afterwards the city lived on its commercial cunning and its prestige as the cultural capital of the western world.

In 146 B.C., the Romans, whose empire had been crawling eastwards for 70 years, replaced the Macedonians as rulers of Greece. They cruelly sacked many Greek cities, but Athens they honoured. Only briefly, in 86 B.C., was their tolerance abandoned. After the Athenians recklessly joined a king in Asia Minor in his war against Rome, the veteran Roman general Sulla stormed the city and permitted the massacre of many of its citizens. But even the stern Sulla was not impervious to the city's past. He finally called a halt to the slaughter, praised the Athenians of earlier times, and announced, "I forgive the living for the sake of the dead."

Julius Caesar, in turn, pardoned the city in 49 B.C. after it had supported his rival, Pompey; he went on to initiate the construction of the Roman Agora, whose marble ruins are still scattered about the Plaka. From this time, too, dates the loveliest of Roman relics, a hydraulic clock called the Tower of the Winds, which stands near by. In 27 B.C., when Augustus became the first Roman emperor, he completed the Agora begun by his grand-uncle. Cultivated Romans now flocked to the city—among them the poets Horace and Ovid; it became the greatest centre of education for the youth of aristocratic Rome.

Roman-ruled Athens enjoyed its greatest prosperity during the reign of the emperor Hadrian. He chose to live in the city from A.D. 120 to 128. Hiring the Greek historian Plutarch as his tutor and guide, he reverently explored the Acropolis and then set out to achieve the impossible: to equal the splendours of the Acropolis on the plain below. He extended the city walls eastwards and there built a multi-columned library, a gymnasium, a pantheon, a triumphal arch, and completed the colossal Temple of Olympian Zeus, which had been started and abandoned six centuries before. His triumphal arch still stands, oddly insipid, above today's whirling traffic. But little else remains except fragments of the Temple of Zeus— a cluster of giant columns, bereft of their body.

A projected royal palace and a gigantic new statue of the goddess Athena command the Acropolis in an architectural plan commissioned by King Otho shortly after he was installed on the throne of Greece in 1833. The scheme to turn the sacred hill into the seat of the new monarchy was eventually rejected—apparently for financial reasons—and Otho built a palace on Syntagma Square instead.

In the peace that the Roman Empire brought, Athens slowly declined. The Romans regarded the city with mixed feelings: with a conqueror's contempt, yet with respect for its culture (which Rome, of course, adopted). But its intellectual vigour was seeping away.

Not even the Roman peace could last forever. Soon after A.D. 250, the ramparts of Athens were rebuilt against the threat of barbarian invasion. In the year 267, the threat materialized and the city was sacked by Goths sweeping west from the Black Sea. The whole fabric of the Roman Empire was loosening and, early in the 4th Century A.D., the Emperor Constantine moved his administration to the city of Byzantium on the Bosphorus, renaming the new capital Constantinople. Slowly the eastern and western halves of the empire, both Christian by now, were drawing apart and, in the 5th Century, the west was overwhelmed by barbarians.

For another thousand years, the eastern half—Greece included—endured as the great Christian empire of Byzantium. In 529, the schools of pagan philosophy in Athens at last closed down. One by one the great temples became churches and the Greek love of philosophy was confined to hammering out the dogma of Christianity in holy councils. But the lodestar and capital of the Mediterranean was now Constantinople.

Athens, by contrast, seemed tainted by its pagan past. The city shrank and changed. Plague took its toll; and, in the 7th Century, Slavic tribesmen, filtering south, percolated into the suburbs and settled there.

For five more centuries, Athens slept. But slowly, in the Europe to the north, a new and belligerent Christianity was growing, and at last it spilled into the Levant in the form of Crusades against the Muslims in the Holy Land. In 1204, the soldiers of the Fourth Crusade, eager for plunder, were deflected from sailing to the Holy Land and attacked Byzantium instead—for Constantinople offered incomparable riches. When the Crusaders parcelled out the Byzantine provinces they conquered, Athens was given to the ruler of Burgundy, Othon de la Roche. As part of the "Duchy of Athens", it knew a modest prosperity and supported a feudal French culture of troubadours and tournaments. In 1311, it was seized by Catalans, who ruled it without distinction for 77 years. They, in turn, were supplanted by a Florentine dynasty whose gentler rule was doomed, towards the middle of the 15th Century, by the spread of a new and formidable power in the east.

Since their emergence from Central Asia in the 13th Century, the Ottoman Turks had bitten their way through the eastern provinces of Byzantium. In 1453, they took Constantinople itself, and three years afterwards they annexed Athens. Thereafter, for close on three centuries, the city languished under the Turks. Not only was the Parthenon turned into a mosque, but the district governor lived in the Propylaea and housed his harem in the Erechtheum. (The stone caryatids were said to have blushed with shame.) To Greek and Turk alike, the monuments of the past were no more than enigmatic phantoms.

But by the end of the 18th Century, the effects of the French Revolution —a world-wide call for liberty—and of Russian collusion with Greece against Turkey, were starting to show. Nationalistic brigands called *klephtes* roamed more boldly through the countryside. Meanwhile, expatriate Greeks in various European countries were undergoing an intellectual Renaissance; revolutionary societies appeared and, by the early years of the 19th Century, the concept of Philhellenism—a romantic love of Greece and a yearning for her independence—had taken hold of many European poets and intellectuals.

The Great Powers at this time, even Russia, were cautious; but their subjects were not. "We are all Greeks," declared the English poet Shelley. "Our laws, our literature, our religion, our arts, have their roots in Greece. But for Greece . . . we might still have been savages and idolators. . . . The modern Greek is the descendant of those glorious beings whom the imagination almost refuses to figure to itself as belonging to our kind, and he inherits much of their sensibility, their rapidity of conception, and their courage." Shelley himself had never been to Greece.

Lord Byron, Shelley's countryman and fellow-poet, was perhaps the

"Maid of Athens, ere we part. Give oh give me back my heart"—so wrote the English poet Lord Byron, portrayed at right in Greek costume, after visiting Athens for the first time in 1809 and falling in love with Theresa Macri, above, his landlady's 12-year-old daughter. His passion cooled when Mrs. Macri offered the girl's hand in marriage in exchange for "a trifling present of gold," but the poet's ardour for Hellenic culture burned bright until he died in 1824 during the war for Greek independence.

most influential Philhellene of all. He, at least, knew the country, and his verses came like a nostalgic trumpet-blast:

> *Fair Greece! sad relic of departed worth!*
> *Immortal, though no more; though fallen, great!*
> *Who now shall lead thy scatter'd children forth,*
> *And long accustom'd bondage uncreate?*

The Greeks themselves made the first important move. In March, 1821, the standard of revolt was raised in the Peloponnese and 15,000 Turks were massacred there by the *klephtes* and peasants. The Greeks proved superior at sea and tenacious in the hills; however, true to their old character, they were chronically divided. European volunteers, Byron among them, went to their aid. Four months after his arrival, Byron died of plague in the besieged lagoons of Missolonghi; but his death immortalized the struggle.

In 1825, the Turks' ally, Mehmet Ali, Pasha of Egypt, landed 10,000 Arab troops in the Peloponnese. During the next two years, his son, Ibrahim Pasha, subdued the peninsula in a hard-fought campaign that did not end until the French Philhellene Colonel Charles Fabvier surrendered the Acropolis in June, 1827.

Now that the Greeks were at their last gasp, the Great Powers stirred into action. On October 20, 1827, in the Bay of Navarino, the combined British, French and Russian squadrons inflicted a crushing defeat on the fleets of Turkey and Egypt. In a single day the Greek cause was won.

Political manoeuvres over a peace treaty and the establishment of boundaries for the new Greece were long and complex, and there was the problem of choosing a new king. The only certainty was the selection of the new nation's capital. It had to be Athens—the "renowned Athens, god-haunted citadel" as the Greek poet Pindar had once put it. The city was an umbilical cord that stretched back through the shame and uncertainty of two millennia to a light of almost unimaginable splendour.

Timeless Oases in a Hectic Metropolis

PHOTOGRAPHS BY MICHAEL FREEMAN

Set amid trees below the Acropolis, the classical Theatre of Dionysus seems a world apart from the modern city across Dionysiou Areopaghitou highway.

No monuments of the ancient world offer more glorious glimpses of the shaping of Western civilization than the ruins centred on Athens' rock citadel, the Acropolis. Most of the remains erected by the city-state that rose to splendour in the 5th Century B.C. have had to be rescued from oblivion by archaeologists: the Theatre of Dionysus (above), for example, lay buried beneath a farmer's wheatfield until excavations began in 1838. As seen in the aerial photographs on these pages, the marble monuments of the classical period—as well as the scattered sanctuaries of later centuries—are now hemmed in by highways, railway lines, office buildings and concrete apartment blocks built during recent decades. Yet the mute eloquence of the relics of the Athenian past manages to triumph over the rising clamour of the jet-age city.

Almost 500 feet above a maze of luxury apartments, the whitewashed 19th-Century chapel of St. George gleams on the summit of Mount Lycabettus.

The Temple of Hephaestus (top) rises almost intact above a deserted Agora, the city's ancient market. At right, runs the Athens-Piraeus railway.

From the massive, marble-crowned Acropolis, bathed in golden morning light, modern Athens fans south to the port of Piraeus five miles away.

The 56-foot-high Corinthian columns of the Temple of Olympian Zeus, dedicated by the Roman Emperor Hadrian in A.D. 132, stand aloof from rush-hour traffic.

3

A Robust Appetite for Enjoyment

Whenever Athenians arrange to meet informally for a social evening, you can be more or less certain that at least one—and maybe all—of them will arrive late. In Athens, no one takes pains to be on time unless the appointment has some obvious professional value. But you can be equally sure that, when all the friends are gathered together and wine has been poured, no one will take a sip before the group has clinked glasses, each to the other, with the toast *"Stin iyia sas"*—"To your health".

To an outlander, the first simple certainty may seem unnecessarily rude; the second an excessive formality. An Athenian, of course, would find explanation easy. Why should he be a slave to time during his leisure hours? As for the ritual toast, has he not learned, like his father and grandfather before him, that wine is to be appreciated with all the five senses: appealing to the palate with its flavour, to the nose with its bouquet, to the eye with its colour, to the tongue's touch with its smooth coolness and to the ear with the companionable clinking of glass?

Such reasoning, I find, says much about Athens and Athenians. In this city, social activity—eating out, drinking, dancing, singing and, above all, conversing—permeates everyday life to an extraordinary degree. Like wine, Athens is to be enjoyed with all the senses; and for its citizens, leisure and pleasure are fundamental elements of day-to-day existence. Time, therefore, is not important.

In most large cities of the world, the inhabitants are increasingly obliged to plan their leisure hours. Such a concept is totally foreign to the Athenian: he takes his pleasure where and when he finds it and enjoys it all the more for its spontaneity. For example, if you were to invite an Athenian to go with you to the cinema a week hence, he might well consider the proposal not only eccentric but downright absurd. How can he possibly accept when he has no idea what other opportunities for fun he might have on that particular evening, or—very much more to the point—what he will feel like doing at that particular moment?

In their social affairs, Athenians tend to rely on a kind of sixth sense—an intuitive awareness of what action is best suited to the mood of the moment. Very often an evening out at a friend's house or a local café will begin with a decision to delay any decision on how the evening should be spent. The unspoken attitude is, let's not rush into anything and make a mistake; let's see how things develop. Meanwhile, we have all the basic essentials for relaxed pleasure: a place to sit, a drink to sip, and friends with whom to exchange news and views. Why introduce an element of anxiety

With an appreciative 100-drachma note stuck to his forehead for safekeeping, a musician plays the tsambouna—an ancient form of Greek bagpipes—during spring festivities on the slopes of Mount Hymettus, a few miles outside the city.

by making plans and then watching the clock to make sure they are kept?

Necessarily, the city's leisure amenities have been designed to accommodate this go-slow approach. Restaurants are geared to meet peak demand from 11 p.m. onwards. Cinemas never bother to advertise starting times in the press; but, as an essential service, they provide a rough synopsis of the story in printed form so that the many untimely arrivals may catch up on the drama unfolding within. Theatres do advertise starting times, but their performances often start 20 or 30 minutes late, and the actors expect the audience to keep drifting in for at least another half an hour after that. Of course, the most celebrated shows—say, a visit by the Bolshoi Ballet—are solidly booked in advance. In general, however, a theatre in Athens will rarely be more. than half full a few minutes before the curtain is due to rise; and after the play has begun, there will be groups of people in the foyer who are still debating whether they should go in or go elsewhere.

The Athenians' aversion to programmed leisure may occasionally infuriate a foreign visitor conditioned to more regulated living, but I have come to regard it as more a blessing than a nuisance. For me, it provides endearing evidence of how they have resisted the ever increasing pressures associated with existence in a modern metropolis. In Athens, more than in any other capital I know, the life-style invites unanticipated enjoyment. The word "serendipity"—meaning the faculty for making happy discoveries by accident—seems particularly apt. Although coined by an Englishman, the 18th-Century writer Horace Walpole, the word could have been designed to describe the Athenians, who in their social life leave so much to fate and make every day an adventure through their relentless curiosity, their spontaneity, and their refreshing facility for communicating with everyone and anyone.

I can perhaps best illustrate this point by recounting just one of many memorable and surprising evenings I have enjoyed in Athens. It began with a midday invitation to join a group of newspaper office workers who were meeting in Kolonaki Square at 7.30 p.m. "We are thinking of going on to the Herodes Atticus," said a young journalist named Georgios. "Perhaps you would care to come along." The great Roman-built theatre was showing an outstanding production, Aristophanes' anti-war play, *Acharnians*, and so I readily accepted. In my over-eagerness, I arrived in Kolonaki exactly on time. No one else turned up before 7.45 p.m.

Why were they late? I didn't ask and they didn't explain. As I have said, the Athenian is not to be made a slave to time; but his habitual dilatoriness goes deeper than that. It can be partly explained in terms of his perpetual concern that no one should get the better of him—in this instance, casting him in the unhappy role of the *koroido* (sucker) who is the first to arrive and is therefore kept waiting. I have also come around to the theory that the tendency to lateness is linked as well to the instinctive gregariousness

of the Greek people. Being the first to arrive means—heaven forbid!—
sitting and drinking alone. I know Athenians who prefer to walk around
the block a few times and then return to see whether someone else has
arrived "first". (There is surely scope for a comedy sketch based on the
confusion of a group of Athenian friends all playing this face-saving
game simultaneously.)

Anyway, on this occasion, I was a willing *koroido*, sitting alone at a
pavement café in fashionable Kolonaki Square. By 8 p.m. everyone had
arrived, without any reference to being late. Introductions were made,
drinks ordered, glasses clinked. Conversation flowed easily. No one took
note of the time or mentioned the fact that the curtain at the Herodes
Atticus (almost a mile away) went up at 9 p.m. and somehow I knew that
it would be unseemly to do so.

Finally, and very casually, thoughts turned to the possibility of making
a move. It was now 8.50 p.m. With a little luck, I suggested, we might
still catch most of the performance of *Acharnians*. Everyone agreed.
But no one displayed the slightest enthusiasm to try. My companions
were far too relaxed to contemplate an eleventh-hour rush by taxi. And
so, less predictably, was I.

Alternative schemes now had to be considered. There began a long
discussion about the respective merits of certain films that were showing
and of popular singers who were appearing at various night clubs. My
companions obviously relished the debate for its own sake. Another hour
slipped by. Then I mentioned that I had never been to the wine-tasting
festival that in summer (from early July into September) is held nightly
at Daphni, six miles outside Athens.

"Ah, that's chiefly for tourists," said Georgios. His tone was gently
derisive and the others seemed to agree. Yet, none of them had been to

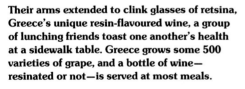

**Their arms extended to clink glasses of retsina,
Greece's unique resin-flavoured wine, a group
of lunching friends toast one another's health
at a sidewalk table. Greece grows some 500
varieties of grape, and a bottle of wine—
resinated or not—is served at most meals.**

In the 1,800-year-old Theatre of Herodes Atticus, a capacity audience of 5,000 Athenians enjoys a performance of The Frogs, a comedy written by Aristophanes in 405 B.C. Classical plays are staged between July and September in the enormous open-air theatre during the annual Athens Festival of Music and Drama.

the festival for several years; and suddenly, after so much division of opinion, they all concurred that it might be something of a novelty. By now, it was 10.30 p.m. and the festival was more than half over, but this did not weigh at all in the final decision to go.

The outing proved to be quite an education. It turned out that Georgios was the archetype of the Athenian chauvinist, the incarnation of an old Greek proverb that says, "If you don't sing the praises of your house, it will fall down on your head." He told me that he loved the Greek Islands, but he could never stay away from the capital for more than a few days— "because I might miss something interesting." Athens, for him, was the centre of the universe—the most exciting city of the present and of the past.

As we headed for Daphni on a main road running north-west from the city, he explained at great length and with inflated pride that we were passing near the site of Plato's Academy; and that near by, too, was the birthplace of Sophocles: the tree-covered hillock of Colonus, which the playwright immortalized in his *Oedipus at Colonus.* "Glorious history is all around," he went on. "A few more miles and we will be starting to climb Mount Aegaleos. It was on that peak, you know, that Xerxes perched on his golden throne and watched us routing his Persian fleet in the narrows between Salamis and the mainland."

The festival, too, had fascinating historical associations. Georgios explained that it was set in the wooded grounds of a famous 11th-Century monastery. The Burgundian Othon de la Roche, first Duke of Athens, was buried here, and the nearby church had some of the finest Byzantine mosaics in all Greece. And, incidentally, did I know that these woods were the setting chosen by Shakespeare for the revels of Theseus, Duke of Athens, in *A Midsummer Night's Dream?*

In fact, Shakespeare did not give a name to his "wood near Athens", but when we reached our destination I could readily accept that the Bard had had something of this sort in mind. The pine woods were more enchanting than any stage set imaginable—a midsummer night's scene

alive with song and dance, as one might expect when thousands of revellers are free to sample scores of different Greek wines at no more cost than the initial entrance fee of 50 drachmas (just over one dollar) and the price of a clay drinking mug.

We strolled along pathways illuminated by myriad fairy-lights strung from the trees, paused in a glade to watch Greek folk-dancing by men and women who swirled around in their colourful traditional costumes: red aprons, white blouses and black-and-gold waistcoats. Then we took a table at the main pavilion, where we could order food and listen to leading musicians and singers appearing on a central stage. Georgios, with typically Athenian quick-wittedness, had purchased a large clay jug in order to avoid numerous trips back to the "bar". It was just as well. Soon after midnight, the casks holding the more popular wines began to run dry.

This phase of our celebrations was brought to an abrupt end at 1 a.m., when the festival closed down. My companions and I immediately found ourselves swept up in a scene of chaos as thousands of wine-tasters simultaneously sought taxis back to Athens. But, then, no one really cared. Time was still inconsequential. We casually started to hitch-hike, and soon a lone Athenian motorist pulled up and offered to take us three miles on our way—as far as a *taverna* (an informal kind of restaurant) where he had a business appointment. Then, on arriving at the *taverna*, he insisted that we should join him in a meal.

I was not surprised by his invitation. Long ago, I had become conditioned to the unrivalled hospitality of Greeks, to similar extravagant gestures by people who often could ill-afford to make them. I was surprised, however, when the stranger's friend arrived and the two men began to talk shop. It emerged from their conversation that we had been given a lift by the millionaire-president of a leading Athenian professional football club. At 2 a.m. he was negotiating to buy a new player for many hundreds of thousands of drachmas out of his own pocket.

What a city! In what other capital, I wondered, would a millionaire stop to pick up hitch-hikers long after dark? Even my companions were surprised, though only because the stranger drove a modest car that completely belied his affluence. It was, they insisted, a very good omen for the evening (they still talked of "evening" at 2 a.m.) and they resolved to make the most of the hours ahead. Reacting again to the mood of the moment, we took a taxi to a night club near Piraeus, and wined and talked and listened to the singers until it was almost dawn.

When my friends finally dropped me off at my hotel and wished me *kalinichta* (goodnight), the sun was rising and the church bells ringing to herald a new Sunday in Athens. Aristophanes' *Acharnians* had been around for 2,400 years. It could wait for another night.

We had 24 hours to recover from that all-night celebration. But do not imagine that it was a very unusual happening or that such nocturnal activity is restricted to Saturday nights. In the centre of Athens alone, approximately 1,500 restaurants and *tavernas* thrive long after midnight. At 2 a.m. this city is far livelier than central London at 11 p.m., and many of my Greek friends will stay out until that late hour *every* night of the week, even though they start work at 8 or 8.30 a.m.

How do the Athenians manage to survive so many late nights? The answer lies in a salutary and time-honoured custom still adhered to by a great many Athenians: the siesta, a prolonged interruption (usually three hours) of the working day. Traditionally, this is the time in the early afternoon for taking the main meal of the day and then going to bed for an hour or so. Nowadays, when the suburbs of Athens sprawl out to the extreme limits of the Attic plain, more and more citizens find it impossible to get home for a proper siesta. They have to be content with eating out and perhaps catnapping for a while on an office chair or at their work bench. Nevertheless, the three-hour break can still have the effect of making one day in Athens seem like two separate days.

Athenians have a highly developed vocabulary for the different periods of the day and the words say much about their philosophy of easy-paced living. *Mesimeri* (midday) does not mean noon but the start of siesta-time —anywhere between 1 and 3 p.m., depending on the timetable at one's place of work. After the siesta comes the *apogevmataki* (little afternoon), a one-hour period of gradually getting back into the full working swing. This is immediately followed by the *apogevma* (afternoon proper), the second half of the workday, which may continue until 8 or 8.30 p.m. We are then into the *vradaki* (little evening), a time to take a stroll or lay loose plans for the *vradi* (evening proper), which begins around 9 p.m. Dinner is taken no earlier than 9 p.m.—and usually an hour or two later. *Nichta* (night) begins at some undefined time after midnight.

Understandably, foreign visitors to Athens make the mistake of presuming that the Greek siesta is simply a reaction to the climate—a

Taking the traditional mid-afternoon siesta that—despite government dissuasion—still interrupts the workday of most Athenians, a boat-hirer in Piraeus harbour (above) naps beneath a canvas canopy. At right, a citizen who has managed to get home for his siesta emerges on his balcony to water a potted plant before heading back to work in the late afternoon.

necessary escape from the midday sun that makes city working life so uncomfortable in summer. But the custom is also widely observed in winter. Basically, this is because the thought of a mere one-hour lunch break is offensive to many Athenians, who respect food and drink—and the concomitant small-talk—as a sensual pleasure too good to be rushed.

Getting attuned to the rhythm of Athenian working life can be extremely difficult for newcomers because no hard-and-fast rules apply. Some workers take their siesta early, others take it late. More confusingly, a growing number of factories and offices have abandoned the siesta altogether or are attempting to do so. Therefore, no standard times can be given for *mesimeri*, for the *apogevmataki*, or for the afternoon proper. When I first visited Athens in 1938, the addiction of the populace to the siesta sent me into a rage: there was so much to do and so little time in which to do it. I remember rushing through lunch by 1 p.m. one day and arriving at the National Archaeological Museum, full of energy, mad for culture, greedy for the gold of Troy.

"Closed," said the guard at the door.

"Why?"

"Siesta," he replied. "Come back at three o'clock."

A national museum closing for a siesta! I couldn't believe my ears. But I soon discovered that this museum's two-hour siesta was one of the shortest in Athens. All the shops were either closing or closed. I stopped at one on Patission Street. While I was examining some shirts on a side-walk rack, the proprietor removed the display and shut his premises with a finality that permitted no appeal.

"Siesta time," he said cheerfully. "Come back at five o'clock."

Four hours out of the middle of the day! What an extraordinary way to run a business! But then all businesses were closed. A somnolence had taken over the entire city. The streets were almost deserted. I saw bartenders drowsing over their bars, waiters falling asleep in rush-bottomed chairs, a man in his kiosk, sitting up but gently snoring. I wandered into the *Ethnikos Kipos* (National Gardens). It was crowded with slumbering Athenians who could not conveniently travel home to take a proper siesta. They slept sitting up on benches or stretched out in the shade of trees—frozen in all manner of postures, as though the place were under a spell, like some enchanted forest in a children's tale.

I followed the winding paths through groves of trees laden with the fruit that the ancients called the golden apples of the Hesperides, but here unromantically labelled *Citrus aurantium*. Water rippled in the irrigation runnels that lined the paths. Here and there, a tortoise was visible in the undergrowth. The sound of running water, the gentle cooing of doves, the heady aroma of orange blossom—all conspired to make me drowsy. I lay down in the cool shade of a linden tree.

It was three o'clock when I awoke, deliciously refreshed by my first siesta. I left the sleeping garden, crossed the broad, deserted avenue of Vassilissis Sofias and walked briskly to the Ministry of Information on Zalokosta Street, where I had business. I was still hopelessly out of step with Athenian time. The concierge reared up in his pyjamas. I felt like a prowler. "Siesta," he whispered, as though afraid of waking the entire ministry. "Come back at half-past five."

By now I had come to realize that the siesta in Athens was more than just agreeable; it was almost mandatory and those who disrupted it could expect to meet trouble. On another day, while resting in the home of friends in Kavouri, a seaside suburb of Athens, I was awakened at 4.45 p.m. by the incessant sound of hammering in a nearby villa. "Clio, call the police," my outraged host said to his wife. Clio called the police. The noise stopped almost at once.

In those days, the Greek siesta could truly be described as the daily afternoon worship of Hypnos, god of sleep, and his son, Morpheus, god of dreams. But it is very different now. In central Athens it is only a lucky minority who can actually get to bed in the afternoon. Most factories have accepted a continuous workday in order to maintain efficient, nonstop production. Moreover, many thousands of Athenian white-collar workers —in ministries, banks and commercial offices—have been compelled or persuaded to give up their siesta and adopt the working hours that prevail elsewhere in Europe. Their numbers are rising year by year and nowadays downtown Athens is noisy with traffic during siesta time.

Even so, the majority of Athenians are not likely to sacrifice their siesta altogether—at least, not during the spring and summer months when the pace of life automatically slackens as temperatures rise. Whether or not they can get home for a proper siesta, they like to unwind in the early afternoon and split their day into two distinctly separate parts. Having become conditioned to this Mediterranean rhythm, I wholeheartedly agree with their resistance to change. The siesta is an essential prelude to enjoying those long, languorous nights in Athens. Without it, this vibrant, most sociable of cities would be a very different and infinitely duller place.

Some writers, in attempting to define the precise quality of the Athenian attitude to life, look back to the roots of Hellenic civilization and suggest that present-day Greeks are, at heart, pagan worshippers of the natural world. I believe that the underpinnings of their way of life are much more close at hand. A practical and materialistic people, inhabitants of a poor and rugged land, the Athenians have learned, through centuries of appalling hardship and oppression, the secret of extracting keen and lasting enjoyment from the simplest of pleasures.

For example, they have no real appetite for the more garish forms of Western entertainment—such neon-lit attractions as the strip-shows and discothèques that have mushroomed in the tourist-trap quarters of Plaka

Customers taking lunch at an unpretentious taverna in the Plaka, an old district beneath the Acropolis, are separated by a wire fence from a nearby archaeological site. Most tavernas are simple affairs, but some have a poet, a singer or a musician to provide entertainment, and others stage a non-stop floor show.

and Piraeus. But for Athenians seeking an enjoyable night out (and that could be *every* night of the week) companionship is absolutely essential and the surroundings are fairly irrelevant—a formula for pleasure that works because these citizens are, as a French traveller once observed, "the enchanters of themselves".

Although watching television is greatly changing social habits, most males—married as well as single—still tend to view with considerable gloom the prospect of relaxing at home. Their homes are rather bare and functional—places for sleeping rather than for entertaining. Wives may be content to take turns at inviting other wives into the home for interminable sessions of poker or *koum-kan* (a kind of rummy), but men prefer to get out as often as possible, meeting friends at the *kafeneion* or *taverna*, or perhaps taking the family to a *zacharoplasteion* (patisserie) for ice-cream, sweets or various gooey concoctions of pastry, honey and nuts.

A *kafeneion* is, literally translated, a coffee-house, but in reality it is much more than that. Day and night, it occupies a vitally important role in the social life of Athens, as a meeting-place and informal club. Athens has several hundred *kafeneions*, which are frequented predominantly, though no longer exclusively, by men. At their tables, for the price of a single cup of coffee, the customer may sit for hours on end, using the place as a kind of public lounge-cum-office—reading newspapers, negotiating business deals, writing letters, playing backgammon or, in some cases, watching television. Many Athenian men go to their local *kafeneion* to get away from their wives and domestic surroundings. Above all, they go there to talk.

The traditional *kafeneion* will serve nothing more than coffee and perhaps sweet pastries. The coffee is called Greek, but (whisper the fact softly in Athens) it is really Turkish—thick, sweet and black, and served in tiny cups that are only half-drained before you come to a muddy and undrinkable sediment. But no matter—the lure of *kafeneions* lies less in what they have to offer by way of sustenance than in their traditional role as an assembly place and debating chamber for the neighbourhood.

Similarly, it is true to say that the hallmark of a popular *taverna* is its social atmosphere, rather than its fare or décor. Tourists are most familiar with the flashy, rooftop establishments of Plaka, with their blinding neon lights and deafening electronic music. Athenians, however, tend to avoid such places; they like plenty of noisy animation, but not so much that it kills conversation entirely. Far more numerous, and for me infinitely more enjoyable, are tiny neighbourhood *tavernas*. Some of them consist merely of a few rickety tables set up each night on a patch of spare ground, with a well-worn path leading to a few casks of wine and the open kitchen of a "restaurant" too small to accommodate more than half a dozen customers indoors. One *taverna* I know, finds extra space by occupying a builder's yard. Every evening, wheelbarrows, spades, hods, ladders and picks are cleared to one side and the spartan surroundings are transformed into a lively night spot.

Some of the more touristy *tavernas* stage a non-stop floor show; but most of them have live music only on a casual basis, if and when some strolling musician makes a call. Whatever their status or pretensions, all *tavernas* worthy of the definition have two things in common: a warm welcome and an open kitchen where customers may look into the simmering pots and choose what they fancy from food that is always Greek, with no concessions to international cuisine.

Athenians take great pride in their culinary arts Drawn into a debate on the respective merits of national cuisines, they are likely to point out that, at a time when the rest of Europe was content to tear at half-raw meat on the bones of wild animals, they were preparing delicacies like roasted lamb with capers and exotic sauces made from herbs and spices. Actually, Greece does not have a great gastronomic tradition of its own. Its modern cuisine has been very much influenced by Turkish dishes—something few Greeks are prepared to admit.

After years of Turkish occupation, it was only natural that Greeks would continue to use many of the Turkish recipes that had become familiar to them. Even now, many Turkish words are used to describe dishes that Greeks claim as their own—like *moussaka*, *baklava*, and *halva*. One dish, stuffed egg-plants, is called in Greek "*imam baildi*", which is a complete Turkish phrase meaning "the Imam swooned"—presumably at the delicious taste.

The range of Greek dishes is modest; and in many instances it is served too cold for Western tastes. But I myself love much of the

Late-night promenaders in the Plaka wend their way along a stepped street, careful to avoid jostling diners seated outside the tavernas that line the route. These eating places begin to serve dinner at about eight o'clock and customarily stay open far beyond midnight.

taverna fare: *souvlakia* (small cubes of roasted lamb or pork and slices of onion flavoured with marjoram and garlic and served on a skewer); *tzatziki* (yoghurt with cucumber and garlic); *kalamarakia* (squid); and, of course, the famous *moussaka*, a minced-lamb dish layered with fried aubergines and topped with béchamel sauce.

A variety of indigenous wines may accompany these Greek delicacies, but the most popular—and one of the cheapest—is *retsina*, a resinated wine possessing a strong taste of the pine resin that is used to line the wine casks and preserve their wood. Since ancient times, the Greeks have favoured this astringent wine for its sharp, clean qualities. Alexandre Dumas, the 19th-Century French novelist and gastronome, complained of Greek wines being spoiled by the introduction of resin; in his *Grand Dictionnaire de Cuisine* he attributed it to an old superstition—"final homage to Bacchus, whose sceptre was a thyrsus tipped with a pine cone." Whatever the origins of *retsina*, it remains uniquely Greek. Californian vintners, adept at producing acceptable versions of foreign wines, have failed to make even a reasonable facsimile.

I cannot resist *retsina*, even though horrified French friends insist that I am poisoning myself with turpentine. To my taste, it is the perfect complement to *keftedes* (meat-balls) or *dolmades* (rolls of rice and meat wrapped in vine leaves), two other staples of *taverna* fare. But *retsina* is certainly an acquired taste; and so, to a lesser extent, is the more potent *ouzo*, an aniseed-flavoured liquor distilled from grapes. *Ouzo* is the equivalent of the Turkish *raki*, a national aperitif almost invariably served with a saucer of snacks called *meze*—chopped tomato and potato perhaps, or olives and some *feta*, a delicious soft white cheese made from goats' milk.

The custom of automatically serving appetizers with a glass of *ouzo*, or even beer, is significant. Just as a Greek will never eat without drinking, so he will hardly ever drink without eating. The idea of standing in a pub all evening sinking pints of beer, as in England, or belting down one whisky after another, as in an American bar, is incomprehensible to him. He drinks sitting down, in company, and always with a tidbit—if only some nuts or slices of melon—immediately at hand.

This partly explains a social phenomenon: the almost complete absence of drunkenness. No matter what the hour or occasion, you are unlikely ever to see an Athenian the worse for drink—unless, of course, you happen to haunt some of the seedier dives down on the Piraeus waterfront, where the boozy behaviour of many sailors is more representative of international custom than Athenian standards. The sobriety that prevails in Athens would be remarkable in any great city of the Western world, but here it seems especially extraordinary. After all, the Greeks were apparently the first people to master the wine-making process. Moreover, they once venerated a god of wine, Dionysus, who, according to mythology, journeyed around the earth to spread his gospel of how happiness might be achieved through drunken oblivion.

Paradoxical though it may sound, the length of Athenian evenings helps explain the city's freedom from drunkenness. Since most *tavernas* remain open until 1 a.m. and some considerably later, alcohol can be imbibed at a leisurely pace. Indeed, with the ever-present diversion of food, conversation and/or music, one does so instinctively. The custom is highly infectious. In Athens, I used to be amazed to find that I had consumed several bottles of wine during a night on the town and was left just pleasantly and mildly mulled.

There is, it should be noted, another important factor that contributes to the lack of inebriation in Athens, and indeed to the relatively low incidence of crime. It is connected with what the Greeks call *philotimo*, a word that has no precise English equivalent but which may be loosely translated as self-pride or self-esteem. Many other Mediterranean countries have recognizable forms of *philotimo* in the unwritten personal codes of honour observed by their men, but nowhere does the concern with personal image influence life in so many ways.

On the individual level, *philotimo* basically involves protecting the ego: don't give others the opportunity of ridiculing you or reason for not respecting you; always beware of losing face, of being outsmarted. Thus, an Athenian is loath to become incapably drunk because it could make him vulnerable to personal abuse or simply diminish him in the eyes of others. It is not a question of morality or etiquette—as can be seen from another manifestation of *philotimo*, the widespread custom among Athenians of pushing in front of earlier arrivals at a bus stop. No self-respecting Athenian, after all, wants to be cast in the role of the sucker, left standing in the street as others ride off in triumph.

Then again, in conversation, *philotimo* may impel an Athenian to speak with assumed authority on a subject about which he has no real knowledge and to stick stubbornly to his views even after they have been destroyed by logic. When Athenians of more-or-less equal stature are gathered together, one often finds several monologues going on at once as individuals blindly persist in trying to hold the centre stage and assert their personalities. In these circumstances, any opinion strongly asserted is better than no opinion at all. To concede an argument entirely is too much akin to admitting inferiority; and truth should never be allowed to interfere with telling a story to maximum effect. Boastfulness is socially accepted as a means of promoting *philotimo*; equally, modesty is becoming in the individual whose reputation is so well established that he does not need to boost his esteem.

Philotimo is a concept no less evident on the collective level, as demonstrated by the Greeks' passionate guarding of family and national honour. In time of war, it inspires fanatical patriotism, and courage and self-sacrifice beyond belief. In politics, as I shall discuss later, it can often be a disastrous, self-defeating force. But for the moment we are concerned with leisure and pleasure; and in this regard it is, for the most part, a likeable trait. To give a very small example of *philotimo* operating to good effect: you will not find a group of Athenians diminishing themselves by haggling over the bill at a restaurant. But there might well be a scramble— sometimes involving heated argument—to commandeer the bill and make the dinner "my treat". They take pride in being seen as generous; at the same time, heaven help the smart alec who insults their ego by calculatedly seeking to take advantage of their good nature.

In emphasizing the lack of drunkenness, I don't wish to give the impression that Athenians are tedious paragons of restraint. Quite the reverse is the case. It is simply that these "enchanters of themselves" do not require the stimulation of alcohol to put them in high spirits. Their senses are honed to such a keen edge that an intoxication of sorts is brought on by atmosphere or ambience. As usual, the Greeks have a word for it. They call it *kefi*, an indefinable exuberance of the heart that is most commonly manifested in *tavernas* by a customer suddenly feeling compelled to get up and perform a solo dance, strangely introspective in nature. Lost to his surroundings, his eyes riveted to the floor, his arms outstretched like the wings of a bird, he moves almost trance-like in a world of his own making. No one applauds, however superb his skill. It is recognized that he dances for himself alone.

My friend Georgios has a simple definition of this state: *kefi* is being drunk with happiness. However, I have doubts about this explanation. Certainly, the *kefi*-induced dancer is impelled by an irresistible feeling of well-being, but that feeling may be based on melancholy as well as joy. He might be celebrating the cherished memory of a long-lost love or merely drifting away on waves of nostalgia. Who knows? The sensuous, transcendent feeling of *kefi* is essentially an individual sensation and the dancing is a form of *katharsis*, an outlet of private emotion.

At its best, the solo dance—the *zeibekiko* made famous throughout the world by Anthony Quinn in the film *Zorba the Greek*—can be spellbinding. But it is much less easy than it looks; all too many tourists arrive in Athens and think of themselves as Zorba almost from the moment they first hear the *bouzouki*, a stringed instrument resembling a mandolin. The result is invariably a travesty of what, in its purest form, is not merely a private ego trip but an almost mystical act of self-expression.

In my opinion, foreigners are unlikely to be transported into a pure state of *kefi*—at least not unless they have some understanding of the Greek language. Good food, wine, music and companionship may put them in the "party mood", but inevitably they miss the message in the songs—especially those known as *rebetika*—which bombard the senses

A shirt-sleeved customer at a taverna near Omonia Square, infected by the night's revelry, leads his companions in a spirited folk dance from northern Greece. Many of the tavernas in Athens cater to Greeks who hail from particular regions of the country—or even particular towns.

In a back-street café, an old man with a bouzouki plays the doleful folk music known as rebetika. The music, introduced to Athens during the 1920s by Greek refugees from Asia Minor, has become standard fare in night clubs and tavernas.

with haunting melancholy and lead the listener into self-reflection. In contrast, every sensitive Greek—which means almost all Greeks—can easily identify with the sensuous melodies and heart-rending themes of *rebetika.* Manos Hadjidakis, composer of the theme music for the film *Never on Sunday,* summed up the common reaction in a description of the first time he heard *rebetika.* He was, he said, "dazed by the grandeur and depth of the melodic phrases. . . . I believed suddenly that the song I was listening to was my own—utterly my own story."

The term *rebetika* derives from *rebetes,* a slang word of uncertain origin denoting a man living a marginal existence on the fringes of established society. In the 1920s, when so many refugees from Asia Minor settled in Athens, the songs of the *rebetes* took root in the under-world of Piraeus. Those plaints, emerging from the waterfront dives, brothels and opium dens, became notorious because they dwelt largely on such forbidden subjects as hashish and prostitution. Their subsequent development into a popular form of *bouzouki*-based music has many parallels with the development of the Blues in America.

I first heard this soul music in the 1950s when a Greek friend named Stavros took me to a *taverna* in Piraeus. The place was practically a dive, but he insisted that this was the proper setting for authentic *rebetika.* Dark, smoky and barely furnished, our *taverna* was crowded with sailors dancing to the haunting 9/4 tempo of the *zeibekiko* played by *bouzouki* and guitars. The customers consumed jugs of wine at an unusually ferocious pace; and when they enjoyed a particular song or the skill of the dancer, they smashed their plates on the concrete floor. The atmo-sphere was one of joyful abandon, and yet—because of one unforgettable piece of *rebetika*—my memory of that evening is more of sadness mixed with faint amusement. The words haunt me still:

I sing from an alien land where it's cold and I grow old.
I can't take it any more, Mother; my body's wearing out.
This alien life is full of bitterness, of misery.
It takes us far from home and wastes us, body and soul.
I'm leaving, Mother. I can't take it any more; I'm coming back
To you, Mother, away from the misery of this foreign land.
But I met a woman, Mother, here in this alien land.
I'm bringing her back: all three of us will try to live together.

The unhappiness of the son forced to emigrate overseas was genuine, and tragically portrayed. Yet, in the very last line, the author of the song could not resist a touch of very Greek irony. How, he asked indirectly, would his wife get along with her new mother-in-law? In Greece, mothers-in-law are notoriously hard to live with and they are the butt of many popular jokes. But it's not always a laughing matter: Athenian newspapers often carry stories reporting the latest incident of a man having murdered his mother-in-law in one of the provincial villages.

At a neighbourhood street market in the district of Neapolis, shoppers jostle past stalls selling eggs, fruit, vegetables and flowers fresh from the surrounding countryside. Such "people's markets" take place on fixed days once a week in every district of Athens.

This kind of simple irony has helped to make *rebetika* extremely popular with bourgeois Athenians as well as with the denizens of the waterfront. The more sordid themes have been abandoned, and the songs now deal with emotional situations familiar to Greeks everywhere: lost love, unfaithful or nagging wives, spiteful mothers-in-law, homesickness, poverty, disease, death. Some are anti-establishment, some are very funny; but for the most part they are intensely sad.

In the night clubs of Athens, I have listened for five hours at a stretch as one professional singer after another has squeezed every drop of emotion from songs of heart-break, treachery and despair. Yet, curiously, the effect is not an overwhelming sense of misery. No one is reduced to suicidal despair by *rebetika*. If there is any painful effect, it is an exquisite pain, as in romantic love, the theme of so many of these songs.

The songs are not too depressing because there is such close harmony of music and poetry; and the music, significantly, has a vitality all of its own. Indeed, some of the melodies have such a lively beat that tourists are misled. Not understanding the words, they expect to see customers leaving their tables to link arms and dance in a line or a circle. In any event, that kind of group dancing is rarely to be seen in Athens except during festivals and at private celebrations.

When reflecting on the Athenians' extraordinary appetite for social pleasures and their constant seeking of sensual stimuli, it is tempting to relate their way of life to the teachings of certain ancient Greek philosophers who expounded hedonistic theories; these sages held that *hedone* ("pleasure") is the sole, or chief, good in life and that its pursuit is the ideal aim of conduct. But really there is no relation; modern Athenians exercise too much discernment and *philotimo*-based self-control to be labelled hedonists pure and simple. I prefer to call them boredom-fighters rather than pleasure-seekers. Boredom is the great common enemy; anxiety comes in a close second.

The endless war with those twin adversaries is most obviously illustrated by the way Athenians continually fondle their *komboloia*. Almost all Athenian men possess worry beads; many have a collection of them— inexpensive sets for daily use, more elaborate ones for keeping at home. "It is a legacy from the Turks," an unusually forthright Greek businessman explained to me (most of his countrymen would not admit that the Greeks ever got anything from the Turks). He then took out what looked like an amber rosary, caressed the beads with his fingers, twirled and clicked them with obvious sensual pleasure. "I do this instead of smoking," he said.

Unlike Catholic rosaries, Greek *komboloia* have no religious significance. They are merely an aid to relaxation, occupying the hands in idle moments and serving to ward off the threat of silence—and boredom—when conversation lags. Despite the assertion by the Greek businessman, I cannot recommend them as a substitute for smoking because I have often seen an Athenian sitting in a *taverna* with a cigarette in one hand and worry beads in the other. Conversely, tobacco cannot take the place of *komboloia*, because worry beads serve a different purpose: for Athenians, they satisfy a peculiarly inborn need for tactile pleasure.

The citizens of Athens have been called the most sensuous people in Europe. It is too sweeping a generalization, one I would care neither to challenge nor support. But certainly they have an extraordinary enthusiasm for touching. Athenians tend to caress almost everything with natural and spontaneous affection—statues, merchandise, their beads, themselves and their friends. "It's as though they're trying to make sure you're real," a foreign student once said to me after he found himself being patted regularly, like some family dog.

Under the Colonels' junta, which lasted from 1967-1974, Mikis Theodorakis, the famed composer, was arrested as a Marxist and imprisoned for 30 months without trial (he was finally released for health reasons). At the time of his arrest, soldiers tied his elbows behind his back, covered his head with a hood, and then beat him mercilessly with their batons. He presumed that his life had reached its end. The faces of his loved ones flashed into his mind, and he reflected sadly that his mother would never see him again. But in this time of agony and terror, his one great concern —as he later recorded—was that "my people will not be able to wash my dead body, caress it, kiss it." It was something that disturbed him profoundly, revealing most of all, it has seemed to me, a deep-felt reluctance to relinquish sensation. Perhaps this reluctance is shared by anyone facing death. But it seems somehow natural that such moving words should be written in a city whose people have mastered the art of enjoying life— literally feeling life— better perhaps than any other people on earth.

Rituals by the Sea

Sunseekers throng the free beach of Varkiza on a Saturday afternoon. Beyond the fence at left lies a beach that charges admission—with no loss of patronage.

Seeking a name for the 30-mile stretch of beaches south-west of Athens, tourist-minded officials inevitably hit upon "Apollo Coast", honouring the ancient god of the sun. The Athenians themselves tend to ignore such classical references—but for more than half the year they crowd the beaches by the thousands. A 20-minute morning swim is part of many a health-conscious Athenian's fitness routine; for others—a fast-diminishing portion of the population—sea-bathing is an easy solution to their lack of a bath at home. The best Athenian beaches charge for admission, providing dressing rooms, showers and gymnastic equipment. However, many beaches are susceptible to a seaborne version of the city's endemic air pollution: factory effluent from the nearby port of Piraeus is sometimes so severe that swimming has to be prohibited.

Seemingly engaged in a ritualistic interchange with a soft-drinks advertisement, a bronzed Athenian pursues physical fitness with knee-bends at Phaleron beach.

Oblivious to a passing cruise ship, a beachgoer takes advantage of the gymnastic apparatus at Vouliagmeni, a beach operated by the Greek Tourist Authority.

Beside a collapsed sea wall separating the harbours of Passalimano and Mikrolimano, a morning bather deals absent-mindedly with an ill-fitting pair of trunks.

Two women follow standard matronly bathing practice at beaches by cautiously testing the water before splashing a few drops on their faces and shoulders.

Using a piece of storm-damaged sea wall as an impromptu chair, a bespectacled Athenian in underwear goes about his bathing routine with at-home serenity.

Modesty is preserved as far as possible by two women dressing after their morning swim—while a male onlooker finds the process of less than absorbing interest.

Three men bob in water whose temperature hovers above 70°F for months.

An offshore buoy normally used for tying up large boats supplies a gently swaying perch for a man determined to do his sunbathing well away from the crowds.

On the beach at Phaleron, a man finds contentment with a good book while his girlfriend is happy just to soak up the sun. The beaches are well served by roads, allowing Athenians to make full use of them on weekends and even during the workday siesta.

4

Saints and Superstitions

Mount Lycabettus is recognized as the supreme observatory on the Attic plain, an 886-foot high look-out point from which tourists can scan every corner of Athens through coin-in-the-slot telescopes. But there is one brief moment in every year when its role is reversed. In the first few minutes of Easter Day, the great fir-clad hill is spectacularly illuminated by myriad candles in the hands of worshippers spiralling down from the diminutive chapel of St. George at its summit. Even the dominant, omnipresent Acropolis is eclipsed, and all eyes are focused on what appears to be the biggest Christmas tree in the world.

It is a truly unforgettable sight. The chapel itself is too small to accommodate a proper congregation for the midnight Resurrection service that is the climax of Holy Week. But as the service nears its conclusion, thousands of Athenians gather shoulder-to-shoulder within the low walls surrounding the church and spread in a great serpentine chain down the hillside; each one clutches an unlighted candle and silently and reverently awaits the moment of universal rejoicing. Shortly before midnight, the dimly lit church is plunged into total darkness, symbolizing the blackness of the grave. Then, exactly on the magic hour, the priest emerges from the chapel and proclaims: "Christos anesti!" (Christ is risen!). "Christos anesti!" The triumphant cry is taken up by the multitude, and each lights a candle from another—sometimes singeing a few heads in the confusion —passing on the light until the summit wears a halo of flickering flames.

On the Attic plain below, tens of thousands of Athenians are celebrating the Resurrection in the same way. In every church at midnight, the door of the sanctuary swings open and the priest appears holding a lighted candle. "Come ye, partake of the never-setting Light and glorify Christ who is risen from the dead," he chants. And the light is passed on to almost every man, woman and child in the city. Church bells everywhere proclaim the Resurrection. Rockets flash across the cobalt sky. An artillery battery fires a 21-gun salute. Ships riding at anchor off Piraeus sound their sirens. Strangers shake hands and embrace in the streets. "Christos anesti!" is the universal greeting, to which the reply is "Alithos anesti o Kyrios!" (The Lord is risen indeed!). Only the sick and the infirm, and widows and those in mourning fail to join in this most joyful event in the Christian calendar.

It is useful to recall that in A.D. 49 St. Paul stood on the Areopagus, a bare rock on the west side of the Acropolis, and proclaimed: "Ye men of Athens, I perceive that in all things ye are too superstitious." He condemned their pagan practices and then reaped their derisive jeers by

Medallion images of Jesus, the Virgin Mary and saints from every period of Christian history crowd the window of an Athens shop that specializes in religious articles. A distinctive feature of Orthodox Christianity—the faith of virtually all Athenians—has been its great number of saints and the intense veneration shown to their pictures, known as icons.

telling them about the resurrection of the dead. How times have changed!
Today, the overwhelming majority of Athenians are Orthodox Christians
and, ironically enough, it is in Greece that one sees the Resurrection
heralded with the kind of national jubilation that many countries reserve
for the beginning of a reign or the end of a war.

Today, the Orthodox Church influences life in Athens to an extraordinary
degree. This is immediately indicated to the visitor by the ubiquitous
priests. With their long, black beards, tall, cylindrical hats and black,
flowing robes, they are noticeable everywhere, standing out like figures
from the distant past who have somehow strayed into the modern city's
brash and busy streets. No public ceremony, great or small, is complete
without their appearance, and even a casual observer soon appreciates
that their role is not merely formal. The State pays the salaries of the
parish clergy and heavily subsidizes the Church's own budget. In turn,
the Church guards the soul of the nation, just as it guards and guides
the souls of individual Greeks.

The Orthodox faith extends far beyond Greece, of course. After Roman
Catholicism and Protestantism, it is the third largest branch of Christianity,
with an estimated 60 to 90 million practising followers, including almost
nine million in Greece. The Orthodox Church originated during the
Byzantine period when Christianity developed two centres, one in
Constantinople, the other in Rome. Until A.D. 1054, the eastern and
western branches of Christendom together constituted "One Holy,
Catholic and Apostolic Church". Then theological and political differences
tore them apart, a schism officially sealed when the Patriarch in
Constantinople and Pope Leo IX in Rome excommunicated each other.
Although the ties between the Orthodox Church and Roman Catholic
Church are stronger today than at any time since the mid-11th Century,
Orthodox rituals and doctrine differ in detail from Rome's, and Ortho-
doxy still refuses firmly to accept the theory of papal infallibility and the
supreme primacy of the Pope.

The Orthodox Church has become a loose federation: it includes four
independent, historic patriarchates—Constantinople, Jerusalem, Antioch
and Alexandria; 10 self-governing bodies located in various countries,
most of them communist; and three so-called autonomous bodies—not
yet fully independent Churches—in Finland, China and Japan. The Greek
Church is a self-governing branch with its own Primate, the Archbishop
of Athens. And Greece is now unique in being the only country in the
world where Orthodoxy is recognized as the official state religion.

Almost every Athenian is baptized in the Orthodox Church (and
usually wears a small Cross throughout life as a reminder) and bears the
name of one of its many hundreds of recognized saints. All marriages of
Orthodox believers are celebrated in church, and remarriage is possible
only if the Church authorities themselves have granted a divorce. In

An elderly priest buys tomatoes in an Athens
street market. For centuries, Greek Orthodox
priests have been known for their long beards
and long hair that is tied up in buns beneath
their hats. But in recent years, some younger
priests in Athens have adopted more fashionable
beard lengths and given up their buns.

theory, the Church permits divorce only on the grounds of adultery, though in practice, other reasons are sometimes accepted. Under no circumstances, however, will the Church grant permission for anyone to marry more than three times.

For the individual Greek, the Church is an intrinsic part of everyday life—not merely an establishment providing places for worship on Sundays and feast days, and the customary services for baptism, marriage and death. On any weekday in Athens you may see people entering churches and buying a candle to light before offering a prayer. Whenever Athenians are about to embark on an important endeavour—buying a house, say, or opening a shop—they may ask a priest to say a blessing. Similarly, when confronted with a major concern, they may light a candle to the appropriate saint—for example, to St. Phanourios or St. Menas if some object has been lost, or to St. Nicholas if the petitioner is praying for a safe voyage over the sea.

Naturally, all citizens especially cherish the saint whose name they bear. I have met quite a number of westernized Athenians who celebrate their birthdays, but this is strictly a self-indulgent exercise, a non-traditional excuse for giving a party and for receiving presents. For the great majority of people, the outstanding occasion for personal celebration is their name-day—the annual feast of their own saint. On this day, it is customary for the individual to remain at home to receive friends and relations who call bearing gifts and bringing a traditional two-word wish: "Many years."

Obviously, a person's name-day, unlike a birthday, is known to everyone. Most Greeks have a diary listing all the Saints' Days, and on those days linked with the most common names—Constantine and George, Anna and Maria—florists, confectioners and bakers in Athens are inundated with orders. The tradition can produce a great social event; alternatively, it can make for a rather boring occasion—a room full of people, half of whom don't know each other, sitting around for hours engaged in polite conversation. Some Athenians prefer to limit celebrations to a select group of invited friends. Therefore, one may see notices in newspapers announcing that so-and-so will not be celebrating his Saint's Day this year—meaning, in effect, that he will not be at home to casual wellwishers.

In addition to the custom of celebrating name-days, a bewildering number of religious feast days and fast days imprint the cycle of the liturgical year on the people's consciousness. There are only three non-religious holidays in the Greek calendar: Independence Day (March 25); May Day; and October 28—*Ochi* (No) Day, commemorating the refusal of the Greek government in 1940 to permit movement of Axis troops across the country's borders. In contrast, there are 10 religious holidays and many more religious dates that are the occasion for half-day closings of shops and offices. Until the 1970s, when a small reduction was made,

Rich Robes for the Liturgy

At the heart of Greece's pervading Orthodox faith is the Sunday and feast-day communion service known as the Divine Liturgy —a chanted pageant performed by priests in splendid vestments that resemble the robes worn 1,000 years ago by courtiers of the Byzantine Empire. The ecclesiastical finery, more elaborate than that specified by any other Christian church, includes a total of six vestments: the long white Alb, or tunic; the narrow Stole, which covers the priest's shoulders; the Cincture, or girdle, which wraps round his body; the Maniples, a pair of ornamental cuffs; the Genual, an apron-like piece of material that hangs over his knees; and the Chasuble, the richly-decorated cloak, worn over the other garments.

Priests own at least three sets of these vestments in various colours, each set made to measure from silks and satins, and embroidered by hand with gold and silver thread. Lest the wearer stray into vanity, he is obliged to recite Biblical verses stressing the holy purpose of his raiment as he puts on each article before celebrating the Eucharist.

A new set of ecclesiastical garments awaits collection in a downtown shop.

Aided by a tailor who specializes in made-to-measure liturgical clothes, a priest picks a fabric from the shop's extensive inventory of resplendent materials.

In a fitting room of one of the several vestment shops near Monastiraki Square, a tailor adjusts a solemn customer's canary-yellow Chasuble.

Greek civil servants were accustomed to enjoying no fewer than 25 religious days off every year.

In this light, Greece may be seen as one of the most religious-minded of all Christian countries. Certainly, at the time of major religious festivals, especially Easter, the Greek Orthodox Church seems an awesome force in Athenian life. But, in truth, the spectacular rituals of Holy Week—and to a lesser degree, of Christmas and Epiphany—say rather more about the Greeks' emotionalism and love of ceremony than the extent of their piety.

Surprisingly, perhaps, the vast majority of Greeks are not regular churchgoers. Indeed, it has been stated that modern Greeks—for all their devout observance of Christian festivals—are as pagan and poly-theistic in their hearts as ever were their ancestors. To my mind, this is an exaggeration. Nevertheless, many distinguished Greek scholars have accumulated evidence to support the claim. For instance, animal sacrifice —a custom basic to pagan religion—is still practised in parts of Greece. In Athens, the foundations of new buildings are sometimes consecrated by the blood of a slain cock. And in some rural areas, a cock, a lamb or a young black bull wreathed in flowers and adorned with lighted candles is sacrificed to commemorate a religious feast or to win favour for some important new community project.

This is not to suggest for an instant that Christianity in Greece is a sham. Quite the reverse. Long ago, the Greeks embraced basic Christian principles and beliefs with the utmost devotion and enthusiasm. At the same time, while remaining within the bounds of St. Paul's "new religion", they have kept alive their simple superstitions and, very subtly, adapted ancient cults to fit in with Christian teaching.

As Professor George A. Megas, the late Director of Folklore Archives at the Academy of Athens, expressed it: "However fervently the Greek people—like most Christian nations—wish to conform with the teachings of the Christian faith, they still retain many beliefs which are not properly Christian: beliefs deeply rooted in the spirit of common man, beliefs inherited from remotest antiquity and often closely akin to the ways of thought of primitive man. The Church has struggled without cease to uproot the myths and customs of ancient worship—by persuasion and enlightenment, threats and punishments. However, man has remained unchanged in this respect: he is still superstitious, credulous, full of fears concerning his earthly and future existence."

Even now, some 1,600 years after Christianity was established through-out the Greek world, St. Paul's chastening of the Greeks for their super-stitious nature still has a considerable measure of validity. The country has an estimated 15,000 professional fortune-tellers, astrologers and spirit mediums. Athenians may no longer consult oracles, but many still try to interpret dreams and to read the future in their coffee cups and playing cards, and in everyday life they recognize myriad omens, ranging from a chance meeting with a priest or a cripple (auguring ill) to an encounter with a pregnant woman (signalling good fortune).

Of course, many of these superstitions are trivial—like common western beliefs about breaking a mirror, spilling salt, opening an umbrella in the house, or having a black cat cross one's path. Greeks share such irrational omens of good or bad luck, and they have many more of their own besides. For example, they say you should never leave desk drawers or closet doors open lest people gossip about you. Fingernails should not be cut on Wednesdays or Fridays, and you should never wash your hair on Sundays. If you leave scissors open, people will say nasty things about you; and if you ever spill wine, put a drop of it on your finger, touch it behind your ear, and say "*gouri*", meaning good luck.

In Athens, one may encounter people who take more sinister super-stitions very seriously indeed. For example, there is an age-old belief that you should never compliment a baby in its presence without spitting on it—very discreetly—to ward off the Evil Eye. Many citizens, educated and uneducated alike, retain a strong belief in the power of the Evil Eye. It is a power that might be possessed by almost anyone—especially a blue-eyed person—and the ill-effects of their hex usually take the form of some malady, perhaps a wasting sickness with no obvious physical origin.

In some villages of Greece this fear of the supernatural has sustained a variety of ancient customs designed to protect the newly-born or the recently departed. At birth, for example, a child is considered to be especially vulnerable to evil spirits seeking to control its destiny. These can be rendered innocuous by fire. Therefore, the hearth in the home of a new-born child should be kept burning day and night. Moreover, from sunrise to sunset the outer door must be kept closed to keep out the *nereids*—no longer sea-nymphs as in Greek mythology, but now half-human earthbound sprites.

Similar precautions, according to folklore, are necessary to ward off the *kallikantzaroi*, a species of goblins, or spirits, who make mischief between Christmas and Epiphany. These small, hairy creatures are supposed to toil all the year round, chopping away with axes at the tree that supports the earth. But every year, when their work is almost completed, Christ is born and the tree grows anew. In their fury, the goblins emerge from the bowels of the earth and cause misfortune for people where they may. Children born at this time are liable to turn into *kallikantzaroi*. To prevent this happening, the mother should bind her new-born child with garlic tresses or straw; alternatively, she could singe the child's toenails. No one without toenails can possibly become one of these monstrous gremlins.

Of course, no educated Athenian would seriously argue the existence of *kallikantzaroi*, or insist that there really is a grim ferryman called Charon who rows the souls of the dead across the river Styx to Hades. Yet there remains in present-day funeral customs a very strong awareness of that concept of reaching "the other side". It is not unusual to see someone whisper in the ear of a dead person or slip a note under the pillow of his bier—a private message to be carried to some deceased relative or friend. Even the custom of placing a coin on the corpse—originally designed to pay the ferryman's fare—has survived.

In ancient times, it was widely believed that corporal disintegration took 40 days. Now, three years are allowed to elapse before a body is exhumed, and the bones washed in wine and deposited in an ossuary. Even so, a memorial service is still customarily held 40 days after the time of death. Since many Greeks still regard complete disintegration as the point at which the dead can find true peace, a ghost is not considered to be the spirit of the dead, but the actual body of someone who has not yet disintegrated. Consequently, it is unusual to find a Greek who has a genuine fear of ghosts.

On a more significant level, the survival of pre-Christian spiritual customs and attitudes can be seen in the Orthodox Church's recognition of 52 major saints and hundreds of minor ones. Many of the Christian saints can be immediately recognized as substitutes for pagan deities. St. Elias, who governs the rain and wind, lightning and thunder, has taken possession of Zeus's mountain shrines, and peasants still invoke his name to send sun or rain according to their needs.

At Eleusis, an industrial town 15 miles west of Athens, the pagan Greeks made sacrifices at the ancient shrine to the corn goddess Demeter, whose daughter Persephone was stolen away to the underworld and kept hidden in darkness like seed corn for half the year. Persephone's annual return to life coincided with the springing up of the new year's crops. Nowadays, Demeter's shrine at Eleusis is the shrine to a Christian saint, Dhimitra. By more than coincidence, local legend has it that Dhimitra's daughter was kidnapped by a Turkish sorcerer on a fire-breathing black horse. She, too, was restored to her mother at Eleusis, thus making the surrounding fields plentiful for evermore.

The popular and heroic St. George, slayer of dragons, may be viewed as a replacement for Ares, pagan god of war, and St. Nicholas has succeeded Poseidon as ruler of the seas and protector of sailors. Furthermore, there is a vast pantheon of entirely original saints serving as healers and protectors—St. Charalambos, who protects Christians against the plague; St. Paraskevi, credited with the power to cure eye-diseases and headaches; St. Barbara, protectress of children against smallpox; St. Vlasios who wards off wild beasts; St. Eleftherios, who eases labour pains in childbirth; and hundreds more. Some of the major saints—such as Constantine, George and Nicholas—seem almost as important to modern Greeks as the gods of Olympus were to the ancients; and all of them, like the pagan deities of old, are to be propitiated with prayers and offerings.

To understand the true nature of religious life in Athens, with its

Votive tokens, intended to express thanks for divine aid, hang beneath an icon (above) in the Church of Metamorphosis in the Plaka. At right, a shop display offers a variety of such emblems for particular thanksgiving purposes: for instance, a token showing a heart may be hung beneath an icon by someone who has recovered from a heart illness, and a token of a car may signify recovery after a road accident.

heterogeneous mixture of semi-pagan and Christian traditions, it is necessary to go back in Christian history to the early 4th Century A.D., when Constantine the Great transformed the small Greek port of Byzantium into the imperial Roman capital of Constantinople. He was founding a Byzantine empire destined to survive for more than 1,000 years before it fell to the Turks. He was also consciously combining two incongruous elements: Hellenic culture, of which Athens was the crowning glory, and the new Christian religion, which Athens was reluctant to accept.

As a pragmatic politician, Constantine saw the advantages of the new religion as a unifying principle, and his Edict of Milan in 313, legalizing Christianity throughout the Roman Empire, was a master stroke of statesmanship and a landmark in the history of religious tolerance. Yet his own commitment to Christianity was, at first, uncertain. During his lifetime, he encouraged the imperial cult of emperor worship and acknowledged two putative heavenly fathers, Jupiter and Jehovah. He also identified himself with Apollo, and when he inaugurated the new capital on May 11, 330, he erected a pillar of porphyry in the forum with his own effigy in the guise of the sun-god at the top.

As for the Greeks, they resisted conversion long after his death, clinging to their pagan traditions with such stubborness that the Christian Church often gained ground only by way of compromises that allowed many of the ancient festivals and ceremonies to be incorporated into the Christian calendar.

At this time, Athens was still the cultural capital of the Greek world. But its prestige and prosperity lasted only as long as its famous schools of philosophy. After 529, when the Emperor Justinian in Constantinople closed down the schools and forbade further teaching of philosophy, the city sank fast to the level of a small and insignificant provincial town. Christianity, with a strong element of eastern influence in its religious ceremony and art, became firmly established.

Throughout the Byzantine Empire, eastern influence was now particularly marked by the veneration of icons—two-dimensional holy images. This form of Byzantine art seems to have derived mainly from the imperial *lavrata* ("portraits") set up in every city of the eastern Roman Empire as objects to sustain the imperial cult of emperor worship. Another source may have been the "mummy portraits" painted on coffins in Egypt at that time. In any case, icons seem to have served as an attractive substitute for classical images of Olympian gods. Their appeal to the Greeks, who like to be able to communicate with God and His saints by way of things tangible, is obvious.

Today the veneration of images depicted on icons is a key part of Orthodox tradition. On entering a church in Athens, a worshipper's first act is to kiss those icons immediately inside the main door. Later he may walk up to the iconostasis—a wall of icons separating the sanctuary from

A street-vendor cooks chestnuts beside a column of the Ministry of Education and Religion, a modern skyscraper built around the Church of Aghia Dynamis (Divine Power). The tiny house of worship dates from the early years of the Turkish occupation (1456-1829), when churches were deliberately unostentatious so that they would not antagonize the Muslims.

An icon-painter in an Athens studio works on a portrait of Christ, following compositional rules that have remained unchanged for centuries. The painting of icons for Greek churches is regarded as a religious vocation, and is often carried out by monks who consecrate their brushes and paints.

the nave—and kiss the icons of Christ, Mary, and the saints and angels. During the service, icons are censed by the priest, and on feast days they are carried aloft around the church.

Almost every Athenian has at least one icon at home, and many people have sizeable collections. These holy images are not idols but symbols. Veneration is not directed towards the icon itself—the stone, the wood and the paint—but towards the divine figure or scene depicted. In the early 8th Century, however, the veneration of icons became so firmly entrenched in everyday worship that the Emperor Leo III launched a full-scale attack against the cult, which to his mind smacked too strongly of pagan idolatory. His soldiers tore down icons from the walls of churches and public places. Icon-worshippers were savagely persecuted, and the iconoclasts (or icon-smashers) continued to have their intolerant way for more than a half-century, until the death of the Emperor Leo IV in 780.

Significantly, it was an Athenian—Leo IV's widow, Irene—who restored the use of icons in the Byzantine world. In her husband's lifetime she defied his command to stop praying before icons in public. Then, as co-emperor with her 10-year-old son Constantine VI, she immediately denounced iconoclasm as heresy. There was something typically Greek in the passionate and fanatical way this Athenian beauty fought for her beliefs. Unfortunately, her personal ambition and ruthlessness became impossibly extreme. When her son sought to overthrow her, she had him arrested and blinded. For five years she ruled alone. Then leading officials and generals conspired against her and banished her to the Greek Island of Lesbos, where she later died.

In 815, encouraged by the Emperor Leo V, iconoclasts regained power in the Byzantine Empire. Controversy raged anew for 28 years, until the veneration of icons was again restored by a woman—Theodora, the widow of the Emperor Theophilus, who died in 843. Today, this restoration is celebrated every year on the first Sunday in Lent, an occasion known as the Feast of Orthodoxy. But it is Irene, as an individual, whom the Greeks best remember in connection with the iconoclastic struggle. This tough and haughty Athenian lady now has a place among the saints of the Greek Church. Her feast day is celebrated on May 5 every year, and you can see an 8th-Century capital emblazoned with St. Irene's monogram in the Byzantine Museum on Vassilissis Sofias Avenue, east of Syntagma Square in central Athens.

This institution—in my view, one of the most attractive museums in the world—was built in the mid-19th Century as a Florentine-style *palazzo* for the Duchess of Plaisance, an eccentric Frenchwoman who loved Greece and went about Athens in a vaguely Greek costume of her own design: a white robe, white girdle, flowing white veils, and upward-curving red Turkish slippers. The museum still retains the intimacy of a private home, and its icon treasures are breathtaking. Among them are a 10th-

An old woman leaves church on Palm Sunday carrying a palm-leaf cross and a sprig of laurel leaves—traditionally credited with curative and protective powers. For the Orthodox faithful, Palm Sunday marks the beginning of a week of solemn ceremonies and strict fasting.

Century crucifixion, a portrayal of utter desolation and sorrow; a 13th-Century St. George, who is a Frankish crusader from his haloed head to the tips of his armoured toes; a 14th-Century winged Archangel Michael, whose moral force fulfils the transcendent function of the icons as an intermediary between the venerator of the image and the holy subject itself; and a rare 14th-Century mosaic of the Madonna and Child.

A marked change is observable in the icons created after the 15th Century. By then, the city of Constantinople had fallen to the Turks, and Greek scholars and painters had fled to Italy, where the long tradition of Hellenic culture flowered into the humanism of the Renaissance. The icons now became freer, less bound by hieratic prescription. One of my favourites in the Byzantine Museum is a portrayal of the Resurrection, painted in 1657; so far as I can ascertain, it was the first Orthodox icon to depict Christ actually emerging from the tomb. Naked except for a swirling loincloth, the Saviour stands on the lid of his sarcophagus, his weight on the ball of his right foot, his left foot crossed behind him as though he were a victorious athlete. His right hand is raised in blessing, his left grasps a crozier as though it were a spear. Waist, thighs, thorax, and biceps are splendidly anatomized with an artistic love of the body for its own sake that would have rendered this version of our Lord perfectly at home on the Acropolis in classical times. This Resurrection is the resurrection of a pagan ideal.

In the wake of Byzantium's fall, it appears that many iconographers who travelled to other lands may have veered from the traditional ways of their religion. The Church itself, however, showed a dogged power of survival in the lands now controlled by the Muslim Turks. Bent on further military conquests, the sultans of Turkey were content to give the Patriarch of Constantinople control over all Orthodox Christians in the Ottoman Empire in return for his personal guarantee of their payment of taxes and their acceptance of Turkish rule. Church officials found themselves forced into politics, and as a result they fell prey to ambition and financial greed. In the majority of cases, a new patriarch had to bribe his way into office, but he could recover his expenses from the bishops by exacting a fee before instituting them into their diocese. In turn, the bishops taxed their parish priests, and the priests taxed their people. Everything was for sale.

Nor was there any stability in the Church. Since an incoming patriarch had to pay handsomely for the office, the Turks soon discovered the advantages of changing patriarchs as frequently as possible. On 105 occasions between the mid-15th and early 20th Centuries patriarchs in Constantinople were driven from office by the Turks; 27 patriarchs abdicated, often involuntarily, and six suffered violent deaths. Only 21 out of a total of 159 died natural deaths while in office. As a result of this extreme insecurity at its top, the Church was divided into bitterly hostile

Playing an Easter game derived from pre-Christian fertility rites, two friends knock together dyed hard-boiled eggs to see which will crack first. The owner of the surviving egg wins the contest—and eats his opponent's egg. In street markets, egg-shaped plastic cages are sold at Eastertime with live chicks (right).

parties locked in a perpetual battle for power and the fruits of power.

Despite the oppression and contempt of the Turks and the corruption and degeneration of the Church itself, Orthodox religion refused to die. The faith had taken root in the hearts and minds of Greek people— fisherfolk in the Aegean islands, shepherds and farmers in the remote mountain villages, shopkeepers and craftsmen in the half-ruined remnants of such great cities as Athens.

These ignorant and poor men may well have resented the money extorted from them to maintain corrupt rulers of the Church, and undoubtedly they felt deep suspicion against the treasonable activities of Greeks who served the infidel oppressors. But they cherished their religion nonetheless, both for its spiritual consolations in their generations of travail and for its continuing assurance of their national identity. Almost despite itself, the Church came to represent their determination to be free again; and, though none of its leaders dared to express such a hope, the people associated Orthodoxy with the great ambition that one day their Christian empire would be restored.

When at last the first rumbles of national rebellion were felt in Greece, the Church was inevitably divided. In Constantinople, the patriarch had become, literally and metaphorically, the captive of the system. At one stage he exhorted his followers to respect the sultan whom God had set over them and to resist the dangerous myth of national freedom—"an enticement of the Devil and a murderous poison destined to push the people into disorder and destruction." But on the Greek mainland, the simple parish priests, the monks and some of the bishops were prepared to follow the devil's enticement. In March, 1821, it was monks of the Lavra monastery near Kalavryta in the Peloponnese who raised the banner of rebellion against the Turks and began the War of Independence.

The banner itself was the sanctuary curtain of Patras Cathedral, delivered to the nationalist insurgents by Germanos, Bishop of Patras. But while Germanos and the monks launched the new independent Greece, the Patriarch of Constantinople baptized it with his blood. He who had urged the Greeks to honour the sultan for the sake of their Church was hanged from the lintel of the main gate outside the Patriarchal palace after Easter Sunday mass—because he had lost control of the Greek people and had finally failed his master the sultan.

Twelve years later, when the war was won, the Orthodox bishops in the newly independent Kingdom of Greece declared their own independence from Constantinople, on the grounds that they could no longer accept the primacy of a patriarch who remained in a city still ruled by the Turks. In making their church self-governing, they broke a very ancient tradition, but they were acting in the spirit of an even more ancient and significant tradition: the tendency of the Orthodox Church to involve itself with politics and the State.

During 400 years of Turkish occupation, the strength of the Greek Church lay fundamentally at the grass-roots level, in its close relationship to village life. Greece, for the most part, was then a peasant society, and the Orthodox priests were themselves peasants. They usually lived and laboured in the villages where they were born and gave spiritual guidance to people whose problems they fully understood.

Today, that tie to the countryside, for so long a vital force in sustaining traditional values and a sense of national identity, is arguably the Church's greatest weakness. Parish priests are still drawn primarily from peasant families—largely because their salaries are too low to appeal to young men from any other section of society. But now this clergy of predominantly rural origin—many of whom have received no more than primary schooling—is expected to serve a people who more and more tend to live in an urban and industrial environment.

In Athens, the educational gulf between priests and parishioners is especially marked, and cruelly so. Priests are largely regarded (particularly by younger people) as being narrow, backward, and hopelessly out of touch with present-day social problems.

Members of the higher ecclesiastical ranks are also suffering a steady erosion of their authority and prestige—partly because of the intervention of the State in the administrative affairs of the Church. The Greek Church is divided into 77 dioceses, each with its own bishop. All the bishops are officially equal, and they constitute the final authority in the Church. But

In the company of a kinswoman, a widow stares at her husband's photograph during a visit to his grave on Good Friday, a day when people throughout Greece go to cemeteries to mourn their loved ones. At right, a priest reads the names of the dead from beneath a sunshade while conducting a memorial service.

the day-to-day administration is left to the Holy Synod, which consists of 12 bishops (appointed for one year only) under the permanent chairmanship of the Archbishop of Athens. Since the Church depends on the financial support of the State, each successive government tends to exert control over the appointment of Holy Synod membership, and usually a major political change will produce an upheaval in the Church hierarchy. During a political crisis in 1917, the Archbishop of Athens and many other bishops were deposed or appointed according to whether they were followers of King Constantine or the Republican leader Eleftherios Venizelos. Fifty years later, when a military junta came to power, the archbishop was immediately removed from office and the choice of his successor was made by a specially chosen Synod, packed with bishops whose politics were acceptable to the military government.

The integrity of the Church has been gravely undermined by the compromises so many bishops have made with the politicians. Some Athenians, especially young people, still despise the Church for having collaborated, however unwillingly, with the Colonels in the seven years of dictatorship. Some also complain bitterly about the consistent failure of the Church to face up to contemporary social issues.

In Athens, not long ago, a sociologist told me: "I find the Orthodox Church the most reactionary, retrogressive institution I have ever encountered in the Western world. There has been no adequate reform movement within the Church. The Catholics at least sit down and discuss all kinds of contemporary issues—birth control, abortion, divorce or whatever. But the Orthodox Church never even contemplates change.

"It's extraordinary. Their moral teachings are violated on all sides. Abortion, for example, is very common in Greece, even though it is illegal. Everyone knows this. But the Church seems almost permissive through its lack of action. It seems unconcerned so long as there is not any new State legislation on abortion that challenges its official doctrines. The Church has maintained its power because it doesn't get involved with political issues unless those issues could threaten its own position. It is concerned mainly with conserving itself."

How far the Church is guilty of failing to face up to social problems for fear of offending its ancient doctrines is highly debatable. But certainly many of its traditions seem badly outmoded. There is, for example, the ponderous and antiquated nature of church services, which usually continue for two and a half hours, sometimes three. These are entirely sung or chanted, without instrumental accompaniment, and in the archaic Greek language of Byzantium, which is largely unintelligible to the majority of Athenian churchgoers.

The congregation is supposed to participate in the liturgy, but in practice the priest and the choir do all the vocal work, and often the priest will be intoning one thing while the choir sings something else. Moreover, the absence of seats in many churches can make worship very wearing. By tradition (though it is no longer strictly upheld) everyone except the infirm should stand—men on the right, women on the left, the children around a dais near the front.

In the circumstances, it seems fortunate that the Orthodox Church—unlike its Roman Catholic counterpart—does not insist on weekly attendance at the Divine Liturgy (equivalent to the Eucharist or Mass). Fortunately, too, discipline within the church is fairly relaxed. Worshippers are not expected to be in church for the start of a service or to remain until the finish; and it is not unknown for churchgoers to wander about during the liturgy and chat to each other.

I am not suggesting, however, that a shorter, revised form of service would counter the dramatic decline in church attendance in Athens. The problem goes much deeper than that. The decline—part of a world-wide trend—is linked more with the break-up of close-knit communities. As one Athenian explained to me: "In this big city, your neighbours don't ask you if you have been to church, and so you don't feel obliged to go any more."

Up to a point, I feel that many Athenians now tend to regard the Church rather in the way they look upon the Acropolis. For much of the time they take it for granted. But they also hold it sacred, and they would not be without it altogether. They turn to it intuitively when in need of comfort or reassurance; above all, they cherish it as part of their national heritage.

Before the 20th Century, and the late arrival of the industrial revolution in Greece, the Church's liturgy had special meaning for everyone because

At the climax of the Resurrection service that concludes Holy Week, worshippers in the Cathedral press forward to light their candles from tapers carried by the white-crowned Archbishop of Athens. The wick-by-wick spread of light among the congregation symbolizes the rising of Christ from the dead.

In the first minutes of Easter Day, fireworks soar over Mount Lycabettus as worshippers with candles stream down from St. George's Chapel on the summit.

it closely mirrored the pastoral and agricultural cycle of the village year. For the shepherd, Christmas was the beginning of the lambing season and for the peasant farmer, the feast of the 12 Apostles fell at the time of the wheat harvest. This hardly applies in the traffic-snarled cosmopolis of modern Athens. Nevertheless, the principle remains much the same. The Church still regulates the great events in the lives of Athenians, and with each religious festival it provides a fresh release for the kind of mass emotional involvement that they love.

This is never more evident than in their approach to Easter, a movable feast that nearly always falls in April. Seven weeks before this Feast of Feasts—one of 13 in the Christian year—the food-loving Greeks are faced with an awesome prospect: 48 days of Lent, during which, according to the rules of the Orthodox Church, they are forbidden on most days to partake of meat, fish, all animal products (lard, eggs, butter, milk, cheese), together with wine and oil. In Athens, most citizens compromise by setting their own restraints and perhaps fasting properly during the first and last weeks of Lent. Yet all the people prepare for the Great Fast as though, like the minority of truly devout Orthodox believers, they were about to subject themselves to a period of the most severe austerity and physical hardship.

The Greeks' idea of preparing for Lent—the longest of four main periods of fasting in the year—is to precede it with a three-week carnival period during which they dedicate themselves to unrestrained indulgence. The second week of carnival time is called Meat-Eating Week—seven days for gorging oneself on slaughtered pigs; the third week is Cheese-Eating Week, a time for concentrating on the dairy products that will soon be taboo. And since organized merry-making is improper during Lent, obviously every night must be party night. Carnival events are staged all over Athens, in the most humble *taverna* and the most opulent ballroom. Every imaginable organization holds a party or its annual ball, and the merriment is wildest of all in the narrow alleyways of Plaka, alive with strolling musicians, revellers in fancy dress and masks, and people dancing in the streets. Here, citizens commonly arm themselves with a two-headed plastic hammer. Each head is fitted with an accordion-like contraption, and the aim is to rap each passer-by on the head and produce an undignified popping sound.

The last weekend before the beginning of Lent is the most riotous time of all. Every *taverna* is packed till dawn, and within the privacy of their homes some men observe a very ancient custom, probably pre-Christian, by dressing up in female attire and performing erotic but essentially humorous dances for the family. The madness ends on the Monday— *Kathari Deftera* (Clean Monday) as it is called—that is the first day of Lent. But once again, the Athenians ease themselves into the new situation: Clean Monday is a holiday during which they may adapt to the austere diet imposed by the Church. To that end, they stampede into the countryside with picnic baskets or find some suitable picnic spot within the city. Even the waste ground surrounding the jumbled ruins of the Temple of Olympian Zeus will be crowded with scores of families dining *al fresco* on shellfish, spring onions, pickles, *halva* (a sweet confection of crushed sesame seeds), and perhaps some wine. They have the Acropolis directly in view, and high above the Parthenon the sky is filled with kites of all imaginable shapes and colours.

These festivities seem almost like Dionysian rites in celebration of primitive gods. But after Clean Monday, everyone recognizes that it is time to subdue passions and serve the one Christian God. The most devout will then limit themselves to water and bread for three days and thereafter survive mainly on meals of boiled beans, raw onions, olives and bread. Many Athenians will fail to keep their self-imposed rules of abstinence, but during Holy Week almost everyone fasts to some degree, and on Good Friday—a day of total fast and abstention from work—the entire city is plunged into deepest sorrow. Flags are flown at half-mast. Evzones carry their rifles reversed. Church bells toll a funeral knell, and at 9 p.m., in churches all over the capital, candlelit processions form to carry the bier of Christ (a flower-decked structure supported on four beams and protected by a canopy) through the streets of every parish. The sense of mourning is universal and extraordinarily real.

I shall never forget my last Easter in Athens. On Good Friday evening, I had a balcony seat in the Grande Bretagne Hotel to watch the principal funeral procession that begins and ends in Athens Cathedral. Darkness had fallen; beneath me, incense smouldered in braziers all around Syntagma Square, so that the flames of candles held by thousands of Athenians seemed caught and suspended like golden fireflies in a pall of perfumed smoke. The centre of the city had become an outdoor church as the funeral cortège, led by the silver-helmeted National Guard, came slowly into view. Two thousand years disappeared. We were mourning a Christ who had been suffering on the Cross that very afternoon.

A 50-piece marching band, with tubas, trumpets and trombones glimmering in the yellow candlelight, played the funeral march from Beethoven's Eroica Symphony. Behind, in slow cadence, marched troops of boy and girl scouts, a contingent of guardsmen, and six Red Cross nurses. Then came another military band, playing the lugubrious measures of Chopin's celebrated *Marche Funèbre*, solemn, melancholy, desolate. More soldiers and sailors followed, and behind them, carrying thyrsus-like electric torches, were lilac-gowned schoolboys immediately preceding a bareheaded priest holding aloft an empty wooden cross. A hush. The people knelt and the square swayed with light as the bier of Christ passed by, borne shoulder-high by white-robed priests.

The Mayor of Athens and the city fathers next came into view, and the thousands crowding the square fell in behind. I joined them, following the procession back to the Cathedral. There, the Archbishop of Athens, crowned like a Byzantine emperor and carrying a gold crozier, led the body of Christ into the inner sanctum beyond the iconostasis. When he reappeared he had exchanged his glittering crown for his everyday black hat. He sat on the Bishop's throne and people surged forward to touch his robes and kiss his hand. After blessing the faithful, he promised his flock the solace of the Resurrection, in the words of St. Paul to the Corinthians: "I will unfold a mystery: we shall not all die, but we shall all be changed in a flash, in the twinkling of an eye, at the last trumpet call. . . . And when our mortality has been clothed with immortality, then the saying of Scripture will come true: 'Death is swallowed up. Victory is won. O Death, where is your victory? O Death, where is your sting?'"

It was midnight. Good Friday was officially over and gradually, throughout the following day, the sorrowful gloom began to lift. All Athens was emotionally involved in this feast of feasts, this drama of dramas. Finally, at midnight on Saturday, the six-day observance of Holy Week ended in an explosion of joy that was as heart-felt as the tears of mourning that had come before. *Christos anesti! Alithos anesti!* He is risen indeed!

Recalling that Easter in Athens, reliving those moments of profound sorrow and wild rejoicing, I am reminded once again how much these people thrive on contrasting sensation as they ride life's roller-coaster of emotional experience. They are quick to respond to changing moods, ever ready to perceive high tragedy or comedy in the smallest occurrence. In this context, the Church may be seen as their spiritual theatre, providing the framework for the greatest productions of human drama. They play the scenes with genuine spiritual devotion and deep respect for Christian traditions. But the general stage management, one feels, is very much influenced by their own acute sense of the dramatic occasion.

5

Man and Woman

Every January 8, something extraordinary happens in the village of Monoclissia, 200 miles north of Athens. On this one day, in accordance with a local custom dating back to pre-Christian times, the sexes reverse their roles. The women abandon their housework, stroll along the streets smoking cigarettes, and take over the village café, where they sit for hours drinking and debating local politics. Meanwhile, by strict tradition, the men must stay at home to mind the children, cook meals and attend to the household chores. Any man daring to venture outside the house is liable to be seized by the village women and subjected to mysterious, unpleasant punishments during a secret ceremony that concludes the Day of the Female Supremacy.

On the face of it, Monoclissia's ancient custom is far removed from the apparently sophisticated world of modern Athens. There is nothing remarkable about Athenian women smoking, drinking in public, driving cars, or competing with men as politicians, doctors, journalists or whatever. In Athens, far more than in remote mountain villages, one can sense that there is some weight to the constitutional clause that says, "Greek men and Greek women shall have equal rights and obligations." Also, Athenian women are more likely to take advantage of their constitutional right to vote than their outlying sisters—although the so-called cradle of democracy did not see fit to establish this principle until the 1950s. (In 411 B.C., the political powerlessness of women inspired the playwright Aristophanes to conjure up the most celebrated of all female demonstrations for his satirical comedy *Lysistrata*; in it, the women of Athens occupy the Acropolis and starve their men of sex until they agree to end their long-drawn-out war with Sparta.)

Athens may have come far in terms of women's rights, but—for all the fine veneer of sophistication and sexual liberation in the capital city—I believe that the curious custom practised by the villagers of Monoclissia still says much about Athenian life today. I also believe that Aristophanes, if he could return across the Styx to 20th-Century Athens, would find much that is unchanged in the relative roles of men and women. Venturing into the *kafeneions* and *tavernas* of the modern city he would hear men talking about women with very familiar disparity and contempt. "Are there persons with whom you have less conversation than with your wife?" Socrates asked a fellow Athenian called Critobulus. To which Critobulus replied: "If there are, there are few." Similar dialogues are to be heard any day in modern Athens. It is commonplace to find husbands confessing

With a flower in his buttonhole and a cigarette clamped between his lips, an Athenian radiates self-assurance as he applauds a passing street parade. Indulged and flattered from birth, Greek men are fierce guardians of their public image and entertain few doubts as to the superiority of their sex.

that the reason they stay away from home as much as possible is to escape a nagging wife. Moreover, I have often heard husbands making open reference to performing their marital duty "once a week"—a slightly more generous attitude than that taken by Plutarch, who recommended that a husband should sleep with a "good" wife at least three times a month "to reduce marital tensions".

To be sure, the age-old phenomenon of male chauvinism is found the world over. But in Athens it is more pronounced than in most great cities. In many ways, Athenian men and women still occupy separate sides of a great social divide. Young men are free—indeed, they are tacitly encouraged—to have sex before marriage; but girls are trained to guard their virginity zealously. Married men may be excused the occasional sexual adventure, yet infidelity on the part of the wife is well-nigh unforgivable. Men are free to haunt *kafeneions* and *tavernas* all hours of the day and night, but it is considered improper for a woman to go to such establishments without a male escort.

A character in Euripides' play *Meleager* says: "A woman should be everything in the house and nothing outside it." That sentiment has much less relevance today, but it still persists. In Athens, only a very small number of married women are employed outside the home—about one out of every 600. It is true that Athenian wives can no longer be described as slaves to housework, since many of them spend an inordinate amount of time watching television or playing cards with each other, usually for money. Nevertheless, men like to keep women in their place—specifically in the home—and husbands will tolerate persistent gambling by their wives simply because it leaves them more free for their own, essentially separate, leisure pursuits.

The deeply ingrained rivalry that sometimes exists between the sexes was driven home to me most graphically when a friend invited me to his parents' house in a poor suburb of Athens. On television we watched an old American movie about a small-town bank clerk who fell heavily into debt through reckless attempts at social climbing on behalf of his family. Finally, the clerk turned to embezzlement and met with inevitable ruin. My friend's parents—like 3 per cent of the Athenian population—were illiterate, and were therefore not helped by the Greek sub-titles. However, they both felt certain they had grasped the basic message.

"Damned women," said the father, when the film ended. "A nagging wife can drive a man to do anything."

"What do you mean?" said his wife. "He was only doing it so that he could spend more money on his mistress." (In the film there had been no hint of a nagging wife nor of a mistress.)

Philotimo—the passionate concern with saving face in public—is, of course, the key factor in the city's male chauvinism. One afternoon I was sitting at a *kafeneion* in fashionable Kolonaki Square. At the next table a

Three young boys find a rich source of fantasy in a parked motorcycle—world-wide symbol of modern masculinity. Whatever the nature of the vehicle, Athenians drive with frenzied competitiveness, and the noise-level in the city's streets ranks among the highest in Europe.

high-ranking officer in the Greek Army was playing backgammon with a friend, who was apparently his lawyer. The friend was trying to persuade the officer not to divorce his wife on the grounds that she had committed adultery. "It would be the better part of *philotimo* to be generous," he argued. "Better to rise above it all. She is a woman and therefore weak. You are a soldier; you should be strong."

The officer thought this over, all the while rattling the dice in his cup. "You are right," he said finally. "I shall be generous. But I shall confine her to the house. She shan't go out again."

A more extreme example of *philotimo* in action is recorded in the annals of the Café Neon, a vast, working-class *kafeneion* in Omonia Square. Here, some years ago, a customer persuaded a friend to accompany him home in order to confirm his suspicions that his wife was committing adultery. The friend did witness adultery. He also witnessed a double murder by the Athenian cuckold. At the ensuing trial, the husband received a long prison sentence for having shot the man, but he was exonerated for the murder of his wife. She had, after all, provoked him by an intolerable wound to his *philotimo*.

The sexual revolution is relatively slow to take hold in Athens because fundamentally this great city remains a village, or rather a congeries of villages. If you take a random sample of, say, 10 Athenian passers-by on the street, you are likely to find two people from the Peloponnese, two from the southern part of mainland Greece, one from northern Greece, the

Aegean Islands and the Ionian Islands respectively, and perhaps three whose grandparents fled from Asia Minor in the 1920s. These citizens still identify strongly with their regional roots rather than with Athens, still tend to divide into sub-ethnic groups and proudly guard their traditional customs, loyalties and standards—including those dictating male and female roles.

An Athenian's first loyalty is to his or her immediate family, headed by the dominant husband or, in the case of separate generations, the father; next, allegiance is owed to the extended family, which embraces all blood relations, however distant they may be. Thereafter, many citizens give precedence to non-relations from their native village or province, favouring them with their friendship and trust, and perhaps business transactions, in preference to "outsiders".

When two strangers meet, professionally or socially, they will very quickly try to discover if they have any roots in common. For example, not long ago, when dining with friends in Plaka, I invited the *taverna* singer to join us for a drink. Within two minutes this man and a lady at our table had established that they both came from Pyrgos, a town about 120 miles away in the Peloponnese; moreover, one of the lady's many uncles was godfather to one of the singer's many aunts. It would be easy to dismiss such an encounter as mere coincidence, but this is to miss the fundamental point: that such "coincidences" are made commonplace by virtue of the Greeks' instinctive habit of seeking to establish and maintain positive links with one another.

In this "small world" of Athens, traditional patterns of social behaviour are not to be lightly abandoned—and the tradition of male superiority dies hardest of all. Just as most Athenian males I know complacently accept their pre-eminence, most women firmly believe themselves to be unfulfilled until they have married and borne a child—preferably a son. It is tempting to exclude the more sophisticated members of Athenian society from this generalization. But even in those ranks one discovers un-suspected prejudices. During my first prolonged stay in Athens, I spent a good deal of time with a charming young couple who had been married about six months. The husband was a business executive and at first I thought him thoroughly westernized in his outlook. Yet, one day I heard him remark to his pregnant wife: "You look wonderful, absolutely radiant. I'm sure it's going to be a boy."

He spoke with great emphasis and genuine pride, leaving no doubt in my mind that in Athens discrimination between the sexes virtually begins in the womb. This 20th-Century businessman would surely have approved the spirit—if not the fact—of Hippocrates' gynaecological prognosis 2,400 years ago: "If a pregnant woman has a good complexion, the child will be male; a poor complexion augurs a female child."

Contrary to all the healthy signs in pregnancy, the first child of this

Players and kibitzers concentrate on a card game in one of the city's thousands of kafeneions—coffeehouses where men spend much of their leisure time.

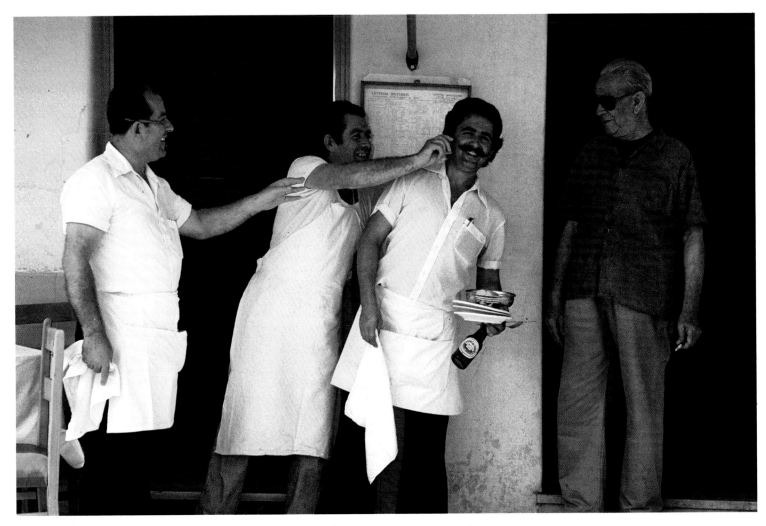

couple turned out to be a girl. Both parents made no attempt to mask
their disappointment. I was subsequently invited to attend the baptism of
Dora, as they named their daughter. She was a perfectly presentable baby,
but at the ceremony everybody seemed mildly apologetic about her
existence. She was anointed with olive oil, then plunged three times into
the *kolymbithra*, or baptismal font, in a rather perfunctory manner. When
she began to howl, her parents looked embarrassed. The Orthodox priest
immediately handed the baby to her godmother, who dried her in a towel,
dressed her in a white christening robe and then whisked her, still
screaming, out of the church.

Three years later I attended the baptism—performed by the same
priest—of Dora's baby brother. As the first son, he had been automatically
named Orestes after his father's father (by tradition, only a second son
may be named after the *mother's* father). Orestes' baptism was an infinitely
more joyous and elaborate affair. The priest began by testing the water
with his index finger and, when he received the child from his *nonos*
(godfather), he kissed the baby on his chubby cheeks. Neither of these
niceties had been accorded to Orestes' sister. Then again, whereas
Dora had been smeared very hurriedly in olive oil, Orestes got a thorough
massage. The priest anointed his nostrils, his ears, his chest, feet, hands—
virtually the whole body.

After the third and last immersion, Orestes came up gasping and bawling
with rage. Parents and godparents rushed to comfort him. They patted him
gently in a towel, fondled and caressed him, kissed his neck, toyed with
his hands and feet, arranged his damp hair in hyacinthine ringlets. All

this loving attention had a magic, tranquillizing effect. The baby cooed in the arms of his *nonos* and, as we walked around the font with lighted candles, the priest proclaimed that Orestes was now immunized against the devil and his works—a speech his sister had not heard.

One compelling reason why most Athenian parents prefer to have a son is the dowry system: "With abundant gold are we constrained to buy a husband," lamented Euripides' Medea. This sigh of woe seems as valid today as it was 2,500 years ago. There still are places in rural Greece and its islands where nubile maidens are decked out on feast days in necklaces, bracelets and head-dresses of old coins that are mounted in silver and gold, the better to lure would-be suitors. In the district of Epirus in northern Greece, the bride goes to her wedding on horseback, carrying jewels in a casket; in Crete, the dowry often follows her to the church on a mule train.

In Athens, the dowry, or *proika*, most commonly takes the form of a small apartment costing the bride's parents somewhere around $10,000. In the event of an upper-class match, considerably more valuable housing might be provided for the newly-weds, and other forms of wealth may be thrown in. Among Athenian shipowning families, for example, full or half-ownership of giant oil tankers has apparently been part of more than one dowry. In 1962, when Princess Sophia, daughter of the late King Paul and Queen Frederika of Greece, married Prince Juan Carlos, now King of Spain, the Greek people contributed the equivalent of $700,000 in taxes as their part of the *proika*.

Naturally enough, Greek feminists are strongly opposed to the dowry system. They argue that it puts women on the auction block, making a mockery of the concept of marrying for love, and that its total abolition is an essential step towards establishing real equality of the sexes. As one leading anti-dowry campaigner has expressed it: "In this country, men chase women for their money and not for the woman's personal worth. The man does not see her as a person. She is an estate, without mind, soul, heart, passion. . . . "

On the other hand, there are plenty of valid arguments in favour of the system, and I have heard them expressed by women as well as by men. In Athens, salaries are so low and rents so high that, without a dowry, most young couples need to work many years before they can afford to make a home of their own; and this is presuming they can both find employment in a city where the labour force far outnumbers the total jobs available.

More persuasively, it is argued that the system gives women a degree of financial protection and greater status. The woman retains title to the principal of her dowry after marriage. Admittedly, the husband may exploit it—in the words of one feminist critic, "spending, investing and doing with the interest as he pleases". Nevertheless, ownership of an

During the complicated ritual of baptism, parents, relatives and friends beam proudly as a male addition to the family is anointed with holy oil after being immersed three times in the baptismal font by a priest. Anointment also takes place before the baby's immersion.

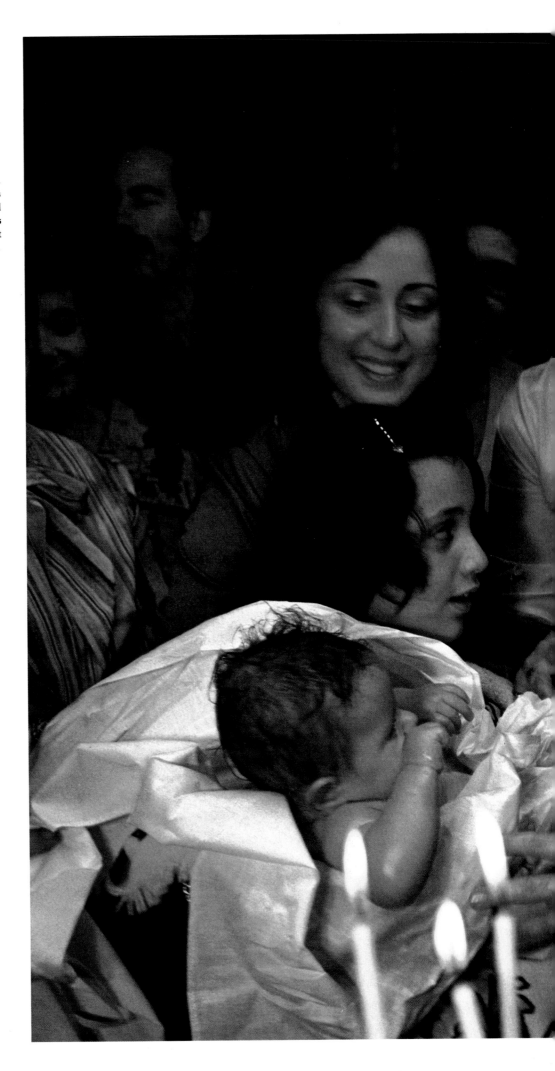

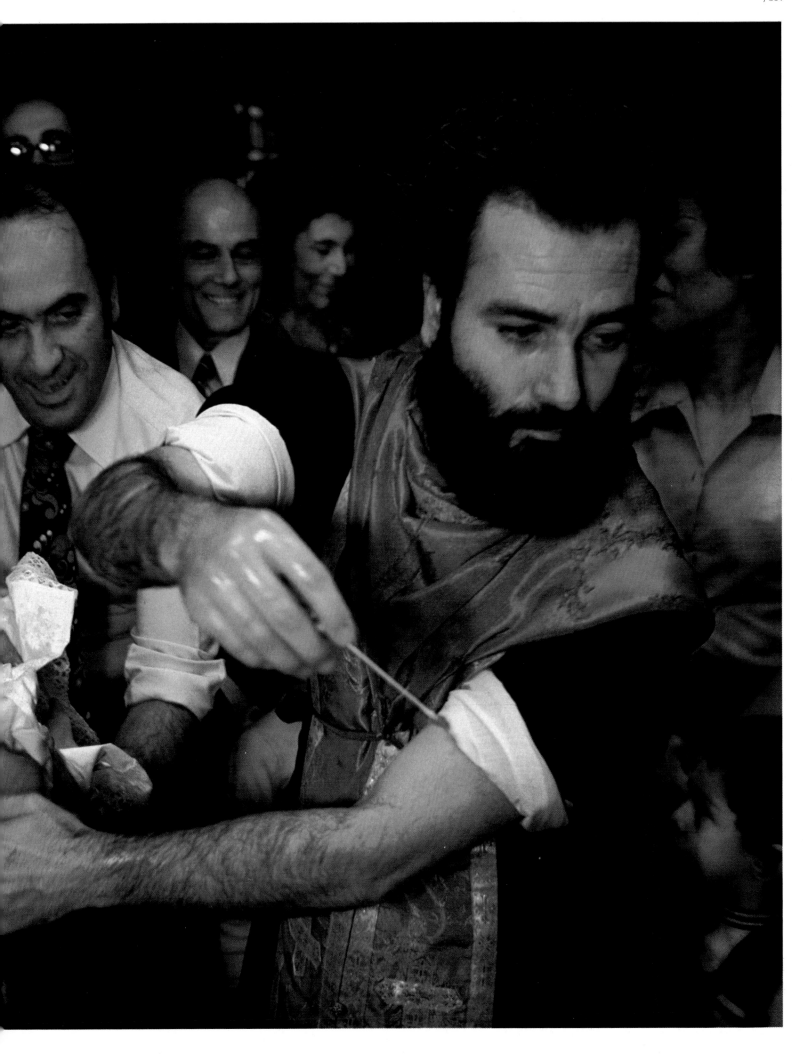

apartment can provide a beleaguered wife with a powerful measure of leverage in her marriage. Indirectly, she has made a substantial material contribution to the union and therefore need not feel that she is an insignificant partner. And if her husband deserts her, she is not left completely destitute, since the dowry is still legally hers.

At first, perhaps with an instinctive touch of male chauvinism, I concluded that the dowry system was marginally justifiable. But now I could never defend it. In economic terms, it means that savings that could be reinvested to increase the productivity of a farm or business are siphoned off to build up a dowry. Moreover, I have encountered too many tragic stories arising from the custom: the devoted daughter who married a boorish shopkeeper she loathed because it pleased her father to ally two family business interests; the proud farmer who had five daughters and who decided that he could reconcile personal honour and economic needs only by emigrating to Australia (he explained: "They say there are rich Greek men there who want to marry a virgin even if she has no dowry.")

I remember especially a delightful afternoon I spent with a Greek friend as guests of a 66-year-old widow and her daughter living in the Athens suburb of Agioi Anargyroi. Our hostess was a great bear of a woman —proud, warm-hearted and immensely strong. She greeted me with a crushing hug and fiercely refused any help in the kitchen as she prepared a meal she could ill afford. When lunch was finished, she emptied the dregs from my coffee cup on to a doily and began to tell my fortune, mischievously concluding with the forecast: "You will become as famous as Byron and your next book will make you a millionaire—and, please, could you remember to send me 10 per cent."

We all laughed. Then, with an air of great seriousness, she emptied the coffee cup of her spinster daughter, Chariklia. "Ah," she began, "your future is very bright. Soon—very soon—you are going to meet a tall, dark stranger. He is very kind and generous, and he will ask you to marry him. You will be very happy."

On the way back to central Athens, my Greek companion explained to me that her friend Chariklia was 36 years old—and that her mother had been telling her fortune regularly for nearly two decades. Always the prophecy began with the daughter meeting the man she would eventually marry. The predicted event had never happened. Chariklia seemed doomed to remain with her mother.

"But that's ridiculous," I said. "Chariklia is not some simple country girl. She's a well-educated, liberated woman. She has travelled abroad. She has an attractive personality, and she has a good job in the city."

"Exactly," said her friend. "And how, without a sizeable dowry, is she likely to find a husband of similar intelligence in Athens?"

In 1957 King Paul and Queen Frederika promoted a new kind of welfare state benefit, a scheme whereby citizen committees all over the country

A young secretary makes use of a public telephone at a news-stand to set up a social engagement. Traditionally, young women cannot go out on dates without the approval of their closest male kin. Although women are gaining a measure of independence in Athens by taking jobs, many of them still arrange dates in secret, owing to constraints imposed by their families.

conducted drives to raise money for a national dowry fund. Each time 1,000 drachmas—then worth about $33—were raised, a bank book would be issued in the name of a baby girl selected by the local committee from the poorest families in the district. When she reached her mid-twenties, the girl would have, with compound interest, enough to buy a few fertile acres and a cow. "The royal couple," one grateful Greek said, "have changed the birth of a girl from a curse to a hope."

In fact, it changed nothing. The scheme failed to catch on and so did a similar dowry-aid programme launched by the military government that ruled Greece from 1967 to 1974. Since then, government policy has leaned towards discouraging the dowry system rather than towards a method of propping it up. But, in reality, the custom transcends legislation. No law can prevent a father from offering his daughter a gift when she marries, and no amount of Women's Liberation argument seems likely to dissuade Greek men from looking for material benefits in a marriage.

In the cities, as opposed to rural areas, the dowry system is no longer strongly upheld by the working class, and naturally it is scorned by many university graduates. But it still has a firm hold among middle-class families. In Athens, a monthly newspaper called *Synikesion* (Arranged Marriage) provides a kind of form chart of the financial attractions available in the marketplace of love. (Sample entry: "Sturdy woman, 45, capable of manual work, virgin with *proika* of 100 olive trees and 20 acres, seeks someone of 50-55 years of age.") In more conventional newspapers one can still read reports about fortune-hunters reneging on a proposal of marriage after pocketing a piece of the dowry, and accounts of a prospective father- or mother-in-law assaulting a man who has thus deceived their daughter. Invariably, the parent guilty of such an attack pleads a defence based on "reasons of honour"—an argument liable to gain a considerable measure of sympathy in any Greek court.

The survival of the *proika* custom is by no means the only reason why the birth of a boy is hailed in Greece with considerably greater enthusiasm than the birth of a girl. Deeply held convictions about male-ness also come into play. It is accepted by society that a man has not truly proved his masculinity until he has fathered a son. By the same token, if a marriage does fail to produce a son it is commonplace to find the husband suggesting that it is his wife's fault. After all, to accept the responsibility himself would be akin to denying his own masculinity.

In their own way, women play an enormous part in perpetuating these attitudes about parenthood. The wife who produces a son feels that she has accomplished her key role in life, and she exudes as much pride of achievement as the father. She immediately rises in stature within her extended family and social circle, and she idolizes her son even while he is dressed in diapers. The mother seeks to control her son strictly by using the age-old weapons of the "weaker sex"—lavishing love and attention upon the offspring and, at difficult times, playing upon his compassion with tears and sighs.

Fathers, who proudly see their sons as extensions of themselves, are naturally reluctant to apply any form of strong discipline. As a result, boys are outrageously indulged and spoiled by both parents. Little girls, by comparison, seem almost invisible. They are upstaged by brothers and, as they become older, they are taught not to make themselves conspicuous because such behaviour would be unfeminine and liable to lessen their attractiveness to the more assertive male.

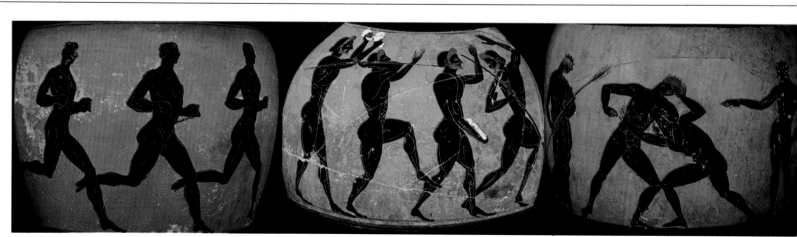

Naked runners in a long-distance event   Contestants in the Pentathlon   Wrestlers, watched by a judge and trainer

I have never ceased to be amazed by the patience with which small boys are suffered. I remember, for example, attending a dinner party given by Athenian friends who had an only child named Emmanuel. It was shortly after Christmas and almost the entire evening was dominated by this five-year-old boy showing off his presents. He began by threatening the guests with a plastic rifle. I affected terror; other adults, foolish enough not to react, received a sharp and painful jab in the knee with the muzzle. Not yet satisfied, Emmanuel then produced a very realistic toy revolver and exploded caps at point-blank range in the faces of guests seated on the sofa. After this he rode his new tricycle through the apartment, barking the shins of anyone foolhardy enough to keep their feet on the floor. No one attempted to restrain this high-spirited brat. After all, he was unique—the only son and heir. He remained the centre of attention until midnight, when he finally fell asleep from sheer exhaustion.

On the infrequent occasions when an Athenian male child is disciplined, the punishment is likely to be half-hearted. I saw this demonstrated in a park one day, when a three-year-old boy threw a stone at his older sister with his parents looking on. His father reproved him with a single whack on the bottom. It was more than the child could stand. He clung, screaming and bawling, to his father's knees. The father relented immediately. He picked up the boy and kissed him on the eyes until joy shone through the tears. Then he swung the child on to his shoulders. Toying with his father's ears, the child continued to ride through the park on his moving throne of privilege, respectfully followed by his mother and his tearful sister, who was told to stop whimpering.

At first, the pattern of indulgence struck me as being positively unhealthy—a sure-fire formula for breeding tiny tyrants. Surprisingly, however, it does not have that result. What counter-balances any possible ill-effects is the example set by the father as the omnipotent patriarch. From an early age a boy becomes aware that he is the heir to this position

A bareback horserace   A javelin-throw from horseback

The Masculine Ideal

To the ancient Greeks, the male human physique was the noblest achievement of nature. Every four years, in a series of athletic contests called the Panathenaic games, the young men of Athens tested their bodies to the utmost as a form of homage to the goddess Athena (a similar athletic festival was held at Olympia to honour Zeus). Victors in the games received jars of sacred olive oil that were decorated (left) with images commemorating masculine strength and grace.

Massed athletes from 12 countries join in callisthenics at the opening ceremony of the first modern Olympic Games in 1896. The revival of the ancient athletic festival was staged in a reconstructed marble stadium originally built in Athens in the 2nd Century B.C. for the Panathenaic games.

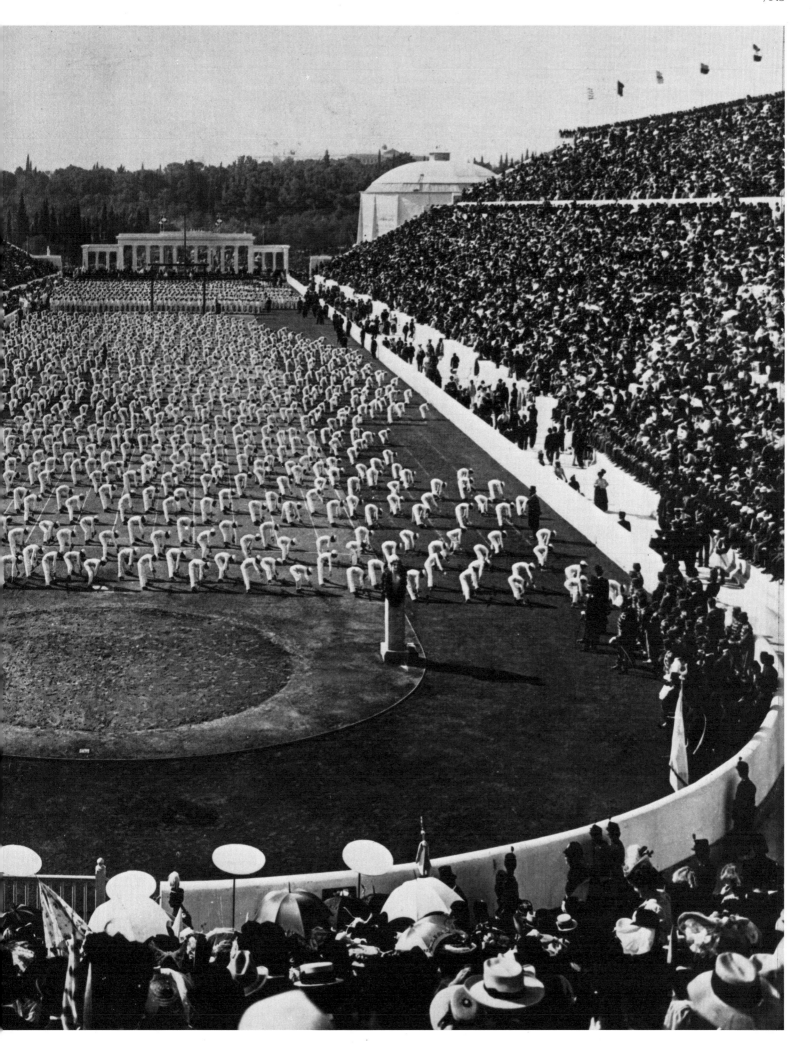

of authority, a prince in the family kingdom. His privileged treatment inevitably fosters a sense of masculine superiority; but as he grows older it also develops in him a remarkably strong sense of responsibility. He will never be called upon to help with the housework: his duties are of a more awesome kind. As soon as he is able, the eldest son will take a share of the father's responsibilities—helping to build up his sister's dowry if necessary and playing a part in guarding her virtue, and upholding the family's *philotimo* in general.

Unlike his sister, he is free to date members of the opposite sex as he pleases. But even this sexual freedom for the male has severe limitations. Since the majority of Greek girls necessarily beware of losing their virginity before marriage, a young man cannot easily gain sexual experience, except in the company of a prostitute or a liberated tourist from abroad. If he sees—or, perhaps, meets within a group—a Greek girl who takes his fancy, he should properly make his initial approach via her relatives: perhaps his father will speak to her father, or his brother to her brother. Then, given family approval, the two may begin to "walk out" without a relative in tow as a chaperon. The girl is still likely to guard her virginity in case the relationship fails to work out; and the boy is all the more aware of the need for responsible conduct, since his family's *philotimo* is now openly at stake.

In Athens, as opposed to rural areas, these strict controls are becoming very much less rigid as more job opportunities become available to women. A daughter can secure a degree of economic independence, thereby easing the burden on her father—and brothers. And, by way of foreign films and tourism, young people in Athens are exposed more and more to the sexual liberalism accepted in many Western countries. But, in the main, they are not properly equipped to face up to the perils involved in such liberal attitudes. No sexual education is provided in the schools. "You simply would not believe how ignorant young people are about sex," an Athenian businesswoman told me; "A great many girls do not even understand what it means to begin missing periods."

With such lack of education, modern contraceptive techniques have not revolutionized sexual life in Greece as they have done in so many countries. Moreover, the Greek Orthodox Church strongly discourages the use of birth-control devices. In any event, harsh economic realities, as well as firm-rooted family tradition, act as a brake on any headlong stampede into the Permissive Age.

For all the inequities and rigidities of the traditional relationship between the sexes, there are compensations for women once they have married. The male sense of *philotimo* is so strong that, when he has a family of his own, he will generally take his responsibilities seriously and guard constantly against damaging the family reputation. Thus, his wife will not worry about him returning home drunk; and if he does take a

A Piraeus dock worker sculls under the bows of one of the steamers used for ferrying passengers and goods between the port and the Aegean islands.

A Hard-working Port

Ever since Athens established itself as a seafaring power almost 25 centuries ago, the port of Piraeus has been a focus for the city's workaday energies. It lies just five miles from the centre of the metropolis sandwiched between the turquoise waters of the Saronic Gulf and the belching factory chimneys of Greece's main industrial zone.

Dominated by the tides of tourism and trade, Piraeus is the central terminal for vessels plying between the Greek islands and is also a major anchorage for the commercial shipping of more than a score of different countries. Fishing, too, is an important local industry, although it now takes second place to the servicing of super-tankers.

Two Piraeus workers line up a hull plank and a third seals the deck as they near the end of their work on a new caique—a fishing boat with a broad beam.

Canisters of calor gas are delivered to a caique, while the tug on the left waits to tow it out to sea. The white glare of the gas lamps will attract fish.

Fishermen relax over the peaceful afternoon task of repairing their nets in readiness for the evening catch.

Afternoon shadows define the barnacle-encrusted hull and propeller blades of a vessel undergoing descaling operations in one of the two dry docks of Piraeus.

mistress, there is the consolation—for whatever it is worth—that he will do so discreetly and never parade his paramour in public.

The focusing of attention on the male throughout his life undoubtedly fosters an overweening sense of masculine pride. But in some ways such pride can be an admirable trait. Athenian men are not prone to a sense of personal insecurity and are therefore that much more able to conduct themselves with a kind of natural dignity. Athenian waiters, for example, provide service in a gracious manner and without a trace of servility.

In certain popular restaurants in Athens it is the custom to summon a waiter by banging a glass with your knife. I resisted this at first because it seemed peremptory and undemocratic. But now I do as the Athenians do. It effectively attracts the waiter's attention and, in normal circumstances, he will respond cheerfully. I say "normal circumstances" because I once dined in Piraeus with a self-willed American girl; and when *she* banged her glass, the waiter looked up and refused to budge. Then I tinkled the glass. He came gladly at once. We were men and, therefore, equals.

There is one common circumstance, however, when the Athenian male seemingly recognizes no equals—not even among other men. It happens when he is seated behind the steering wheel of a car. I have yet to encounter an exception to this rule. In particular, I recall a hair-raising journey from central Athens to Piraeus in a chauffeur-driven Mercedes belonging to one of the richest women in Greece. The lady—I will call her Mrs. Spyros —was a very dignified and elderly matron, and I automatically presumed that she would have a well-disciplined driver. Nothing of the kind. Her chauffeur's name was Orpheus and, like so many Athenian drivers, he was always competitive, cutting in and out of lanes, tailgating and shouting insults at everyone he passed. Mrs. Spyros was obviously terrified, but her mild remonstrances served only to spur the man on to greater recklessness. "He drives much too fast," she explained, "but what can I do? He will never pay any attention to me. I am only a woman."

I told her, quite frankly, that we were in real danger of joining Orpheus in the underworld, and that the only logical solution was to sack him and hire a more responsible driver. "Oh, I couldn't do that," she replied. "He has a wife and two children. Unfortunately, the children are both girls, and that is very frustrating for the poor man."

Significantly, Orpheus became a model chauffeur the moment we arrived at the Piraeus Yacht Club. He leaped out of the car, opened the door for Mrs. Spyros with a grand flourish, and offered a helping hand, as though he were some court chamberlain welcoming royalty. When we left him, he was admiring his own reflection in a wing-mirror of the car. He straightened his tie, stroked his moustache, and then began to flick the gleaming mirror with a feather duster that he wielded like a conductor's baton. There is a strong element of narcissism in the Athenian male, and especially in any Athenian wearing a uniform.

In classical Athens, when men were not marching off to war they gave fullest vent to their aggressiveness in the Olympic and Panathenaic Games. Competition was restricted to men; women were not even permitted to watch. Nowadays, the nearest equivalent to those ancient Games is professional soccer. The sport is not barred to female spectators, but basically it is an all-male preserve in which the Athenian brand of *machismo* achieves its most vivid form of expression.

An official of the Panathenian Athletic Association took me to my first soccer match in Athens. The game was between two of the 18 clubs in the National Greek League—Panathenaikos of Athens and Ethnikos ("The Nationals") of Piraeus—and it was played in a soccer stadium near the centre of the city. "Tell me where you like to sit," asked my host beforehand. "With high society or *hoi polloi*?"

"High society," I replied, believing that, in any society the less wealthy soccer fans are liable to be concentrated behind the goalposts. Sure enough, thousands of *hoi polloi* were jammed into bleacher seats at the far ends of the stadium while I had a perfect position opposite the halfway line. All of us, however, were separated from the field by high iron bars with in-curving spikes, the kind that confine animals in a zoo. "It's to keep the fans from assaulting the referee," my companion explained.

A reserved ripple of applause greeted the appearance of the blue-shirted Ethnikos team. Over the loudspeaker system someone began to announce their names and numbers. But there was no hope of hearing this information; the white-shirted Panathenaikos players were running on to

Supporters of the top professional soccer team in Athens, Panathenaikos, exult as the team scores a goal in their stadium near Mount Lycabettus. Soccer is by far the most popular sport in Athens, attracting a volatile audience made up almost exclusively of men.

the field amid a deafening roar from the partisan crowd and the explosions of firecrackers set off in the stadium and thrown from adjacent apartment buildings. Then, immediately before the kick-off, the roar of the crowd dwindled to muted anticipation. The moment of silence was broken only by the strange clicking sound of the fans nervously flipping through their worry beads. I looked at the *komboloi* of the executive-type gentleman sitting next to me. Each bead bore the picture of a Panathenaikos player. As he caressed them, he reverently intoned his own litany of hero-worship: "Domazos, Kamaris, Anntiodes, Grammos, Constantinou. . . . "

It was as though he were praying for victory on the eve of a crucial battle. Yet there was no need. The outcome was apparently entirely predictable: all the betting—illegal but widespread—was confined to forecasting the home team's eventual margin of victory. By half-time, Panathenaikos was leading 3-0, a modest score that belied their almost total domination of play. I would gladly have abandoned the one-sided contest at this stage but I did not wish to offend my host, and in any event there was no way out. The gatemen had locked all the exits so that they could watch the match themselves.

Midway through the second half, with the Athens team ahead by 4-0, the seemingly impossible occurred. The Panathenaikos goalkeeper, perhaps in a moment of lapsed concentration, allowed Ethnikos *to score!* Any cheers for the Piraeus team were at once drowned in a torrent of abuse for the erring defender. Although the match was obviously not in jeopardy, the goalkeeper, in despair, flung himself on the ground, rolled about dramatically, and then poured dust on his head. It was like an echo of the ancient Panathenaic Games after which, according to the poet Pindar, defeated athletes skulked about the back streets of Athens, hiding their faces in shame.

My neighbour solemnly detached the player's picture from his worry beads. The goalkeeper, he suggested, had probably accepted a bribe to upset the betting odds (such corruption does indeed happen in Athenian football). Meanwhile, the "high society" section around us was shouting insults to the effect that the goalkeeper's parents had never married, and that he was the worst traitor to the city since General Alcibiades had helped the Spartans to defeat the Athenians in 414 B.C. The enraged *hoi polloi* were less subtle. They stormed the iron bars, shook their fists and tormented the luckless goalkeeper with the dirtiest words in demotic Greek. But the ultimate expletive, the supreme insult, was the estimate that the player was nothing more than a woman.

His arms pugnaciously akimbo, an Evzone lieutenant barks an order at his men during a rehearsal parade in the courtyard of their barracks in central Athens.

An Elite Corps of Guardsmen

A detachment of guardsmen, their eyes narrowed in the glare of the midday sun, move with somnambulistic ease through the familiar routine of drill practice.

Evzones—the fancifully dressed soldiers who stand guard outside the Presidential Palace and Tomb of the Unknown Soldier—are familiar figures in Athens, but few visitors realize they belong to a unit with a long fighting history. In the 1820s they emerged from mountain villages to help win independence from Turkey. They were subsequently chosen as royal bodyguards, largely because their uniforms were based on the Greek national costume (*evzone* literally means "well-girt"). However, they continued to serve in combat: Ernest Hemingway, reporting on another conflict between Greece and Turkey in 1922, recalled the shock of seeing dead men in "ballet skirts". Today, their duties are mainly ceremonial, but their status in the Army remains high, and men from other units consider it an honour to be asked to join this élite corps.

A guardsman polishes the brass buttons of his fermeli, using a cardboard shield to avoid staining the richly embroidered material underneath.

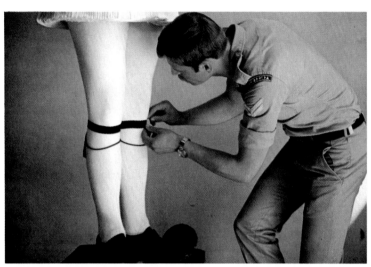

Helping one of his men prepare for parade, an Evzone corporal adjusts a garter.

Standing back, he checks that the skirt-like foustanella is hanging smoothly.

He fits the krossia—an apron of silk straps—around the guardsman's waist...

... and bellies out the sleeves of his shirt before handing him his tunic.

Preparing for Parade

Dressing for parade is an elaborate ritual that requires the advice and assistance of a critically minded fellow guardsman. Over white stockings, the Evzone puts on a huge-sleeved shirt and a kilt—known as the *foustanella*—whose 400 pleats take up 25 yards of cotton. Other distinctive elements of the uniform include pompommed slippers, called *tsarouhia*, and a thick woollen tunic—the *fermeli*—that is embroidered by specialist members of the corps.

Two Evzones guarding the Tomb of the Unknown Soldier are dwarfed by the Old Palace—now seat of Greece's Parliament—which rises above the monument.

Exchanging posts, the sentries pass in front of the Tomb's simple cross and slab. The marble memorial was erected in 1928 to commemorate all Greek war dead.

Guardsmen at the annual Easter festivities line up for a formation dance.

A Day of Barracks Revelry

Evzones are as fond of celebrations as any Greeks, and one of the high points of their year is Easter Day, when they commemorate the end of Lent with a banquet at their barracks near the Old Palace. With their families and a few honoured guests—among them the President of the Republic—they dine on lamb grilled over charcoal and enjoy exultant displays of traditional dancing.

With their white-sleeved arms stretched out like wings, the men entertain their guests with the tsamikos—a spirited country dance from the Peloponnese.

After taking down the national flag on the Acropolis—a task they perform every Sunday—Evzones stroll past the Parthenon on their way back to their barracks.

6

A Passion for Politics

"We do not say that the man who takes no interest in politics is a man who minds his own business," Pericles once declared. "We say that he has no business at all." For more than 2,400 years this dictum has been the unofficial motto of Athens. Indeed, the citizens of this contentious city have taken it so much to heart that I have often wondered how they manage to find the time or energy for any business other than politics. The turbulent atmosphere of the *kafeneions* and *tavernas* rivals that of the parliament building in Syntagma Square; and the Athenian who does not have his own detailed plan for national salvation seems to be about as rare as a Turkish tourist on the Acropolis.

"The truth is that it is very difficult to work seriously in Athens, and to concentrate on becoming successful and rich," Mrs. Helen Vlachos, the influential Athenian newspaper owner, recently observed. "There is something in the climate that curbs every ambition not connected with politics." Some would say that a major cause of climatic disturbance is the Athenian press itself. More than 15 daily newspapers are published in the city, and all are avidly searched for choice morsels that can be regurgitated during the coffee-house debates. No newspaper editor believes in allowing his readers to go hungry and each day's journals are therefore laden with appetizing exposés of ministerial intrigue, juicy revelations of midnight meetings behind locked doors, and delectably apocalyptic forecasts of coups, crises, confrontations and catastrophes.

Ranging from the far right to the extreme left of the political spectrum, most Athens papers are united only in their refusal to recognize the inconvenient distinction between news and views, and in their readiness to sacrifice what is tasteful for what is tasty. Even Mrs. Vlachos spices the highly literate columns of her respectably conservative *Kathimerini* (Daily) with gossip about the private lives of public figures.

As the favourite targets for newspaper comment, politicians are not averse to airing their views about the Athens press, which one former minister has described as the "yellowest in the world". Critics complain that, in their quest for the sensational, the newspapers are more concerned with personalities than policies, reporting political differences as if they were Athenian soccer matches. In fairness to the press, it must be said that the politicians provide plenty of scope for such treatment.

It is more than 130 years since the Greek parliament was first constituted and for much of this time its members have pursued no cause more devotedly than that of self-interest. For the most part unencumbered by

Flanked by government ministers (left) and journalists, a member of the Greek parliament addresses his colleagues from the speakers' dais. Although the 300 deputies are elected under various party labels, Greek politicians tend to be individualists, giving as much weight to personal impulse as to party loyalty.

ideological commitment or party loyalty, they have moved in whichever direction the scent of power has taken them, creating a hectic kaleidoscope of fissiparous groupings, factions and alignments. The politician who has found his ambition thwarted in one party has quite happily thrown in his lot with another, and governments have risen and fallen with the regularity of a powerful tide. Between the end of the Second World War and the start of the military dictatorship in 1967, for example, no fewer than 41 governments whirled in and out of office, some of them failing to survive beyond even a couple of months.

Although political life became much less turbulent after the restoration of democracy in 1974, personal inclination has always counted for as much as party loyalty. The success of a party leader depends not only upon his skills as a statesman, but also upon his ability to play the role of benevolent godfather to his importunate followers. Indeed, to be a godfather—literally as well as figuratively—is the first rule of the political game.

Even in the increasingly cosmopolitan atmosphere of Athens, the family remains the bedrock of social relationships and the chief task of any aspiring politician is to become a member of as many families as possible. He does this by acquiring a peculiarly Greek kinship status known as *koumbaros*, which ensures his acceptance as one of the family in the sight of God. He can achieve such status by acting as best man at a wedding, thus becoming godbrother to the groom, or by standing as godfather to a child, which also makes him godbrother to the child's father. Either way, the *koumbaros*—as he is called—is deemed to have entered into the mutual and indissoluble obligations imposed by true blood relationship.

Left-wing students deliver some amplified oratory outside Athens Polytechnic, a traditional stronghold of political radicalism. Ever ready to practise what they preach, the Polytechnic students in 1973 led a protest demonstration that helped rouse world opinion against Greece's military government—but at the price of 25 deaths and scores of injuries.

Thus he is entitled to the loyalty and the votes of his brothers in God, and they are equally entitled to his protection and support.

The trouble with this kind of arrangement is that it can be ruinously expensive as well as politically rewarding. Every wedding or baptism calls for an appropriate gift from the *koumbaros*, and the assiduous politician can find himself shelling out for as many as two or three hundred ceremonies a year. This is nothing new. As Dr. William Miller, Athens correspondent of the London *Morning Post*, observed at the turn of the century: "One prominent statesman, who had been more than once Prime Minister, has lost all his fortune in politics; another much of his; and all the leading men become poorer by going into parliamentary life. One of the most costly items of a candidature is the duty of standing godfather to the children of constituents. M. Ralles [a leading politician of the day] is said to have a thousand godchildren in Attica, who are doubtless one source of his vast popularity there; another politician, temporarily out of Parliament, is said to have two hundred; and every godchild costs the candidate from 30 to 50 drachmas at least, often far more."

The politician must be responsive, not only to his brothers in God, but to every constituent seeking his help. Irrespective of party labelling, he is regarded primarily as a dispenser of favours—and the more favours he dispenses, the more votes he is likely to win. This does not mean that he is automatically open to bribery, since personal honour, or *philotimo*, makes a crucial if somewhat hazy distinction between simple horse-trading and downright corruption. Nor does it mean that he lacks political ideals. But it does mean that his eye for the main chance must be as sharp as that of any Piraeus shipping tycoon.

As well as being instantly and personally available at all times, the politician must be ready to arrange jobs for those who are unemployed, shelter for those who are homeless, hospital beds for those who are sick, scholarships for those who are ambitious, and visas for those who are emigrating. And if he is a lawyer, as Greek politicians frequently are, he must be willing to plead *gratis* for impoverished litigants. In effect, he must contrive to be everyone's benevolent godfather, combining the solicitous aura of the priest with the brash charisma of the super-salesman.

Why, I used to wonder with Anglo-Saxon naivety, should anyone bother with such an arduous role when it was possible to play at being prime minister simply by stepping inside the nearest *kafeneion* or *taverna*? Since a political career appeared to offer little except Homeric toil, financial sacrifice and a guaranteed formula for ulcers, why was Athens as thickly strewn with parliamentary candidates as ancient ruins? Now I know that politics is the major entertainment industry of Greece, whose citizens believe that the golden highway to stardom and success leads directly from the dusty parliament building in Syntagma Square.

But what is it that gives Greek politics—and politicians—their box-office appeal? The answer lies, I think, in the curiously competitive nature of Greek society. Writing of his fellow Athenians more than 2,000 years ago, the historian Thucydides noted that: "Any idea of moderation was just an attempt to disguise an unmanly character; ability to understand a question from all sides meant that one was totally unfitted for action; fanatical enthusiasm was the mark of a real man."

Thucydides would be unlikely to reach a different conclusion today. The Greeks are the most gregarious people I know, but they are also the most fiercely individualistic, investing their social relationships with a gladiatorial zeal that often leads to rivalry and even violence. They seem to share the same basic approach to life as the demonic drivers of downtown Athens; they are continually alert for potential challengers and permanently oblivious to the dangers of head-on collision. Their most urgent craving is for the thrill of competition—and nothing satisfies this craving so well as the tooth-and-claw contests of the political arena.

The perpetual discord of modern Greece has been compared to the continuous rivalry of the ancient city-states. Certainly, the results have been just as disastrous. Little more than a century and a half has passed since Greece achieved its liberation from the Turks, yet in that time it has suffered 10 major military *coups d'état* and a savage civil war, as well as a foreign occupation. The struggle for independence had hardly begun before the Greeks were indulging their age-old passion for internecine strife. Within months of the 1821 uprising, they had established no fewer than three bitterly contending "national assemblies"; and by the time independence was finally secured in 1829, many Greeks had died fighting one another as well as the Turks.

The first luckless leader of the infant Greek state, Ioannis Capodistrias, was assassinated in 1831, at which point the three protecting powers—France, Britain and Russia—insisted on appointing a monarch to rule over their fractious protégé. Prince Leopold of Saxe-Coburg declined the Greek Crown, predicting that: "Whoever becomes King of Greece had better keep his bag packed," and the choice eventually fell upon young Prince Otto of Bavaria. Since Otto (now restyled Otho I) had not been chosen by any of the warring Greek factions, he had few friends among them. More important, he had few enemies, a fact that made the opening years of his reign agreeably, if deceptively, tranquil.

The tensest moment occurred on December 7, 1835, when a British warship suddenly put out of Piraeus and made full steam for Nauplia (Navplion), the small Peloponnesian port that had served as Capodistrias' provisional capital. The Athenians immediately assumed that an insurrection had broken out in Nauplia and one can imagine their disappointment on learning the true reason for the speedy British departure. King Otho had simply decided to abandon his customary Bavarian uniform for

Avid for political news, Athenians crowd to buy their lunchtime papers. More than a dozen dailies, ranging from far right to ultra left, are published in the city.

the Greek national costume, and, since the best tailor was still in Nauplia, the British had been dispatched to fetch him post-haste to Athens.

The king's willingness to change clothes was rather less important for most Greeks than his ability to change frontiers. The protecting powers had deliberately restricted the size of the new state, believing that the smaller Greece was, the less trouble she would cause. In fact, the powers could have devised no policy more calculated to bring about the consequences they sought to avoid. By leaving the Greeks of Epirus, Thessaly, Macedonia, the Aegean Islands and the west coast of Asia Minor under Ottoman rule, they created a time-bomb of nationalist sentiment that was primed to go on exploding well into the 20th Century. This sentiment translated itself into what was known as the "Great Idea", an incendiary notion of national fulfilment encompassing nothing less than the birth of a new Byzantine Empire centred on Constantinople.

No one espoused the Great Idea more ardently than Otho, who spent much of his time vainly inciting Greeks elsewhere to throw out their Turkish masters and link up with his tiny kingdom. But any popularity he gained by exploiting national sentiment was increasingly outweighed by resentment at his autocratic style of government. The veterans of the War of Independence felt particularly aggrieved by their exclusion from power and in September, 1843, they engineered Greece's first modern military coup. An infantry battalion of the Athens garrison compelled the king to grant a constitution and set up a national assembly.

In theory, Greece became a parliamentary democracy; in practice, it remained an absolute monarchy. Otho simply vetoed any legislation he did not like, and used the right of ministerial appointment and dismissal to ensure that the government was run by his own nominees. Such tactics were effective against the elderly and comparatively unsophisticated veterans of the liberation struggle; but by the 1850s a younger and much more formidable set of politicians was appearing on the scene. Their training ground was the University of Athens, which had been opened in 1837 and stood only a short distance from the royal palace. The juxta-position of the two buildings prompted a caustic comment from one choleric old warrior of the independence war. Looking from the university to the palace, he said: "This house will eat that house!"—a prophecy that was largely to be fulfilled.

As well as generating renewed fervour for the Great Idea, the students of Athens University also stirred up fresh agitation against the king. Inspired by the libertarian ideals of the French Revolution, they bombarded the Athens press with manifestos calling for the violent overthrow of the existing régime. "A revolution without blood is like a battlefield without dead men, music without harmony," proclaimed one characteristically lurid tract. "The revolution must be baptized in blood."

The agitation reached new intensity in 1859, when the Italians launched their struggle for independence against Austria. Having waged their own such fight, the Greeks felt a natural sympathy for the Italians; but Otho supported his fellow German, the Austrian Emperor. Greek students demonstrated their indignation by trying to assassinate Otho's Russian consort, Queen Amalia, and in 1862 a number of provincial military garrisons staged unsuccessful revolts. In October of that year, students and intellectuals fomented a more general uprising, and this time Otho was forced to surrender his throne.

Having disposed of one foreign king, the Greeks immediately urged the protecting powers to find them another. The task was not easy, but the choice finally fell on 18-year-old Prince William George, second son of the King of Denmark. He was crowned King George I of the Hellenes, not King of Greece as his predecessor had been. The Greeks were delighted with the amended title, since they took it to imply that all Hellenes, irrespective of national boundaries, were now officially subjects of the Greek Crown. A further cause of jubilation was Britain's decision to mark the new king's accession by ceding the Ionian Islands to Greece.

In the opening months of his reign, a much more liberal constitution was adopted and some sanguine spirits managed to convince themselves that democratic rules would lead to democratic behaviour. They did not retain this conviction for long. Whenever the politicians were not busy bribing or intimidating electors, they were actively obstructing or undermining prime ministers, with the result that between 1864 and 1908 Greece had an average of nearly one general election every two years and a new administration every nine months.

Preoccupied with the day-to-day struggle for survival, governments had little time to grapple with the irksome minutiae of administration. "All the advances made in Athens in recent years are due almost entirely to personal initiative," wrote Henri Belle, a French visitor to the capital in 1874. "The Government does almost nothing to assist these private operations, in fact very often does what it can to obstruct them. The streets are badly kept up, obliterated and eroded by rains that wash away the earth and uncover enormous boulders that jolt the carriages to bits. Certain streets are quite impassable. In many places, and even in the richest quarters, the pavements are so badly graded that at night one risks breaking one's neck twenty times over.

"Boarding schools, hospitals, asylums and high-schools have been founded in too great quantity and often (it must be admitted) as much out of vanity as patriotism. An Athenian will donate a fat sum to erect one of these establishments without reflecting that there already exist several others empty and disused. What he wants for his building is size and his name in gold letters on the front of it; what shows is all he cares for."

In spite of these gloomy observations, M. Belle was by no means pessimistic. He detected "a fund of national energy in all this movement

In a painting commissioned by General Makriyannis, a leader of the Greek War of Independence against Turkey, Athens is shown besieged by Turkish troops.

Although the nine-month siege ended with the surrender of the Greek garrison in May, 1827, the Greeks went on to win their freedom two years later.

which, once it is well regulated and well controlled, will provide a powerful support to a government that is truly patriotic and intelligent." Unfortunately, the governments of the following half century were to show a rather greater capacity for patriotism than intelligence and the fund of national energy was squandered in a series of futile attempts to transform the Great Idea into glorious reality.

The chief apostles of Hellenic expansionism were the students and graduates of Athens University, many of whom came from Greek-speaking territories outside the kingdom. "It is among these Athenian graduates, the doctors and lawyers of 'unredeemed Greece', that the flame of patriotism burns most brightly," wrote Dr. Miller of the London *Morning Post,* "and we can, therefore, scarcely wonder that no punishments are meted out to students who indulge in political demonstrations. . . . But if the University of Athens is a centre of Hellenism all over the Balkan Peninsula and yet further afield, it is none the less a terror to statesmen."

The Great Idea faced its first major test in 1897, when an insurrection in Crete was followed by a declaration of the big island's *enosis,* or union, with Greece. The Turks reacted predictably and the Greek government mobilized for war. While the king's younger son, Prince George, headed a naval expedition in defence of Crete, Crown Prince Constantine led an army across the northern frontier into Turkey. But the ill-prepared Greeks were no match for the highly trained Turks and, after only 30 days, the Greek campaign ended in humiliating defeat. Not only was Greece required to pay war reparations amounting to 100 million gold francs, but she was also obliged to cede frontier territory to Turkey.

While the nation reeled under the shock of military defeat and financial ruin, the politicians plunged into a further round of anarchic feuding. Duels were often fought as a result of riotous parliamentary debates and on one occasion the scuffling of rival deputies became so intense that an ink-pot fell into the holy water provided for the opening ceremony. Bitter partisanship was not confined to parliament. Visiting a hospital at Piraeus one day, King George's Russian-born wife, Queen Olga, suggested that a patient in whom she was especially interested should be moved to another bed she deemed preferable. She was told that this would not be possible because two of the political parties had made a compact, dividing the hospital between them; and the new bed she had designated was the preserve of that political party to which the patient did not happen to belong.

The febrile political atmosphere of Athens was hardly eased by frequent eruptions of gunfire. "The law forbids the carrying of firearms," noted Dr. Miller, "but the law is one thing and the practice another. Most of the people in the cafés wear revolvers and, since the irregulars of 1897 sold their arms, they have been far too cheap. At election times and at Easter there is much reckless firing in the streets and there are many casualties;

A large A for "anarkhia"—(anarchy)—daubed near the plaster cast of a classical bust at Athens Polytechnic, serves to publicize one of the many competing groups of student militants.

for the Greek loves to show his joy by the discharge of ball cartridges on high-days and holidays, and does not always look where he is shooting. I remember once at Olympia, on Easter morning, the cook of my hotel produced a Mauser rifle, loaded with ball, and let fly at random; and an Athenian paper, commenting on the butcher's bill of the Easter festivities, remarked that 'more Greeks than lambs had been slain'."

A decisive turning point in the history of modern Greece was reached in 1910, when Eleftherios Venizelos became prime minister. By building up an alliance of Balkan states powerful enough to wage war against the Turks, Venizelos succeeded in doubling his country's territory and population in only four years. The gains included Epirus, Macedonia and Venizelos' own homeland of Crete. Venizelos then laid claim to the Greek-speaking areas of Asia Minor by siding with the Allies against Germany and Turkey in the First World War. In 1919 Greek troops entered the city of Smyrna, on the west coast of Asia Minor, and it seemed as if the Great Idea was about to be fulfilled. But Turkish nationalists led by Mustafa Kemal Pasha—the future Atatürk—rallied against the Greeks, and in September, 1922, Kemal's army swept into Smyrna. The city was burned to the ground and every Greek who managed to survive the Turkish massacre fled to the sea and set sail for the Greek mainland.

According to one Greek historian, the fall of Smyrna represented an even greater tragedy than the fall of Constantinople. "The Turkish conquest of 1453 did not result in the uprooting of the Greek race from the European and Asiatic regions where it had dwelt since the dawn of history," he has written. But the Turkish conquest of 1922 "uprooted and swept all the Greeks, not to mention the Armenians who shared their fate, out of Asia Minor and eastern Thrace, where they had been settled for centuries, and deposited them across the Aegean, never to return."

The burning of Smyrna spelled the end of the Great Idea. It also marked the start of more than a decade of turmoil. Kings, premiers, presidents and dictators trooped on and off Greece's political stage like clamorous prima donnas in an interminable operetta. It requires a statistician rather than an historian to calculate the number of upheavals that afflicted Greece between 1922 and 1936; but according to one reliable estimate there were "nineteen changes of government, three changes of regime . . . seven military revolutions or *coups d'état* and innumerable minor acts of sedition due to the constant intervention of military juntas in the government of the country."

The political merry-go-round finally came to a halt in 1936 with the emergence of yet another military strong-man, General John Metaxas. In April, 1936, the Greek parliament voted him the power to rule by decree and then obligingly adjourned itself for "five months". It did not meet again for 10 years. The threat of a Communist-inspired general strike convinced the king that Greece was on the verge of revolution and Metaxas had no difficulty in obtaining the monarch's consent to the establishment of a fully fledged dictatorship. Political parties were banned, constitutional liberties suspended and parliament dissolved for an indefinite period. As Plato had warned the uncompromising and faction-ridden Athenians of his own day: "The excess of liberty, whether in states or individuals, seems only to pass into excess of slavery."

Although Metaxas admired the authoritarian regimes of Nazi Germany and Fascist Italy, he was not prepared to see Greece become a mere appendage of the Axis powers. He tried therefore to steer an uneasy course between the dictators and the democracies, declaring Greece's neutrality when the Second World War broke out in September, 1939. But eight months later Mussolini entered the war on Hitler's side and the Greeks realized that their own involvement was only a matter of time.

I returned to Athens in the autumn of 1940 as a visiting professor of English and spent the long, hot evenings discussing only one question: how long before Mussolini makes his next move? Italian troops had already occupied neighbouring Albania and none of my Athenian friends had the slightest doubt that Greece was marked down as the next target.

At dawn on October 28—a date now celebrated in Greece as a national holiday—the Italian Ambassador banged on the door of General Metaxas' house at Kiffissia. Dressed in pyjamas and dressing gown, Metaxas listened impassively as the Ambassador reported that it was necessary for Italian forces to occupy certain strategic positions within Greek territory. Although he had never been a popular figure, Metaxas now spoke on

Welcoming May Day in typical Athenian style, a pair of youngsters have decked themselves and family car (bottom) with wild flowers. As in other cities, left-wing activists stage rallies on this traditional labour holiday—but it is one of the few days in the year when most Athenians forget about politics. Instead, they flock into the countryside to picnic and gather flowers.

behalf of the whole Greek nation. He replied simply: "This means war."

The Ambassador had not even had time to transmit Metaxas' response before Italian troops began crossing the Albanian border into Greece. Faced by a common enemy, the Athenians forgot their political differences and rushed to the second-hand shops of Hephaestus Street to buy guns and uniforms left over from earlier wars. I remember my students chanting the national anthem, as stirring on this occasion as it must have been in 1821, when it helped to spur the warriors of Greek independence:

> *Yet behold now thy sons*
> *With impetuous breath*
> *Go forth to the fight*
> *Seeking Freedom or Death!*

A strange communal joy gripped Athens as her sons marched north to join the beleaguered Greek army at the Albanian frontier. "The worst that can happen is that you get killed," one of them told me. It was in this spirit of heroic defiance that the ragtag Greeks exploded the myth of Fascist invincibility, hurling back Mussolini's troops and pursuing them deep into Albania. Although Metaxas died of natural causes in January, 1941, the Greeks remained unyielding in the struggle. Only the intervention of the Germans in April turned the tide against them. German troops entered Athens on April 27 and three weeks later King George and his government fled to exile in Egypt after making a desperate last stand on the island of Crete.

With most of the prominent Metaxists and royalists in exile, the enslaved Greeks had to look elsewhere for political leadership. It was quickly provided by the Greek Communist Party. Although numerically tiny, the years of repression under the Metaxas regime had accustomed it to clandestine activity, and by September, 1941, its highly disciplined cadres had succeeded in forming a resistance organization known as the National Liberation Front (EAM). Taking good care to disguise its Communist parentage, EAM had no difficulty in recruiting members from among those thousands of patriotic Greeks who were seething for a chance to hit back at the invaders.

One of the earliest and most daring gestures of resistance was the work of a young Athenian Communist, Manolis Glezos, who tore down the swastika flag from the Acropolis. There was little opportunity of following Glezos' inspirational example during the first terrible winter of occupation, when 2,000 citizens in Athens alone were dying each day from starvation. But with the coming of spring, 1942, the resistance campaign began in earnest. As well as organizing strikes, demonstrations and sabotage operations in Athens, EAM also set up the National Liberation Army (ELAS) to carry on guerrilla warfare from the Pindus mountains.

The Communist leaders of EAM, however, were not concerned solely, or even primarily, with resisting the Germans. Their main aim was to secure such an overwhelming monopoly of power that no other faction would be able to challenge their supremacy when the war ended. ELAS was therefore directed not only to fight the common enemy but also to bring to heel a number of other guerrilla groups that had been organized in the spring of 1942. In a grim replay of the factional fighting that had accompanied Greece's war of liberation against the Turks, ELAS began systematically wiping out any resistance fighters who refused to join the Communist fold. So successful was this ruthless campaign that by April, 1944, the only remaining rival to ELAS was the National Republican Greek League (EDES), which clung to a small pocket of territory in Epirus.

Having absorbed or destroyed all other potential opposition, the Communist leaders of EAM/ELAS were now free to carry out the second stage of their plan: the establishment of a "people's" government in Athens before Allied troops arrived on the scene. Astonishingly, they chose instead to join in a government of National Unity headed by a republican politician, George Papandreou, and agreed to place their armed forces under British military command. As a result, the Allies were able to achieve an almost bloodless takeover of Athens and most of Greece in October, 1944, as the Germans withdrew northwards.

Just why the Communists should have decided to change tactics with the prize of absolute power almost within their grasp remains a mystery. They may have been bowing to Soviet pressure or they may have calculated that it would be easier to subvert than oppose the Papandreou government. Whatever the reason, it soon became clear that they had made a serious error. The influence of Communist ministers on the government proved negligible and when Papandreou ordered the disarmament and disbandment of all guerrilla formations, the leaders of EAM/ELAS rapidly reverted to their original policy of seizing power by force. Fighting broke out in Athens on Sunday, December 3, after police had fired on left-wing demonstrators in Syntagma Square. Strong units of ELAS had already moved into the suburbs and, within two weeks, the greatly outnumbered British troops and Greek government forces were squeezed into a small, defensive perimeter in the city centre.

The English cartoonist, Osbert Lancaster, who was serving with a British army unit defending the slopes of the Acropolis, has described his bird's-eye view of the embattled city. "The usual deafening hubbub of Athenian life—the clanging of trams, the shrieks of the street-vendors, the crowing of backyard fowls—which in normal times is here audible as though detached from its background and existing, as it were, in a void —was stilled and the prevailing quietness was emphasized rather than broken by the continuous machine-gun fire in the streets immediately below, the detonations from the direction of Patissia (where the proletariat were blowing up houses to form street barricades) and that peculiar sound, half whistle, half rending calico, which shells make as they pass immediately overhead. Somewhere beyond Omonia Square a group of buildings was on fire, probably a petrol dump, as the tall column of smoke was oily black against the snow of the distant mountains; behind the Theseon, mortar shells fell with monotonous regularity on a corner house by the tram-stop, sending up yellowish-white clouds that hung in the air, round and compact, for a full five minutes before dispersing.

"On the Acropolis itself a group of trigger-happy gendarmerie lounged with an assumed nonchalance by the lower entrance; alongside the Themistoclean wall a pile of cartridge cases indicated where until very recently a machine-gun had been emplaced; in the empty museum a few grubby plaster casts surveyed an accumulation of military debris. Over all towered the Parthenon, its clear unequivocal statement in no way blurred by the barricades hastily erected from fragments of its pillars and caissons, its own internal rhythm uninterrupted by mortar fire or rockets."

Although desperately short of food and supplies, the defenders of Athens managed to hold out until the turn of the new year, when the arrival of powerful British reinforcements from Italy swung the military balance in their favour. After almost six weeks of bloody house-to-house fighting, a ceasefire came into effect on January 15, 1945. The battle of Athens had cost 11,000 dead and damage to property estimated at $250 million. At a peace conference held in February, ELAS agreed to surrender its arms and the Greek government promised to hold elections and a plebiscite on the controversial issue of the monarchy.

For the Greeks, there now seemed to be only two possible alternatives: the Communists or the king. The royalists won a decisive victory at the elections held in March, 1946; and six months later, 69 per cent of the electorate voted in favour of King George II's return. Alleging that these unwelcome results had been procured through fraud and intimidation, the Communists tried once more to take over the country by force. Although the latest rebellion was aided by Greece's new Communist neighbours to the north—Albania, Yugoslavia and Bulgaria—it received little support from the Greeks themselves. A further setback for the insurgents was the announcement in March, 1947, of the Truman Doctrine, under which the Greek government received massive financial aid and military supplies from the United States.

The fate of what the Communists called the "Third Round" was sealed not by President Truman, however, but by Marshal Tito of Yugoslavia. In June, 1948, Tito broke with the Soviet Union and a year later came his decision to close the frontier with Greece. Neither Albania nor Bulgaria could make up for the loss of the rebel supply bases in Yugoslavia, and in October, 1949, Communist resistance finally collapsed. The direct cost to Greece of three years of savage and unremitting civil war was 150,000 casualties and the destruction of what little was left of the country's administration and economy.

British troops keep a watchful eye on Communist guerrillas captured during the so-called Battle of Athens, a civil convulsion in the winter of 1944-45. The battle began on December 3 when the Communists tried to seize power from the incumbent republicans following the withdrawal of German occupying forces from Greece, and it raged unchecked until British reinforcements swung the tide in favour of the government six weeks later.

But the indirect cost was even higher. At least 100,000 Greek Communists fled to safety across the northern frontiers. Another three-quarters of a million people either fled from their villages to escape the fighting, or were forcibly uprooted as government security forces chased after local Communist units. As a result Athens and other large Greek towns became more desperately overcrowded than ever. So great was the nation's self-inflicted anguish that it drove the writer, Nikos Kazantzakis, to remark that "Wolves don't eat each other, Greeks do."

While the nation struggled for survival, its politicians indulged in yet another furious round of musical chairs. Between 1945 and 1952 there were more than a score of different governments with an average life of 150 days. "Is it really unavoidable," asked the newspaper *Kathimerini* two years after the end of the civil war, "that nothing sound, honest and straightforward can be done in this country?" In their frustration with the old political parties, the Greeks turned to General Alexander Papagos, who had led the Greek army against the Italians in 1940 and against the Communists in 1949. Projecting the image of a Greek de Gaulle, Papagos formed a party called the Greek Rally—after de Gaulle's *Rassemblement Français*—and won a landslide electoral victory in October, 1952.

Papagos' elevation to prime minister marked not only the starting point of Greece's post-war economic recovery but also ushered in a decade of political tranquillity unparalleled in all the previous 120 years of independence. It was, of course, too good to last. In 1965 Greece's popular new king, 24-year-old Constantine, became embroiled in a furious row with his aged but volatile prime minister, George Papandreou, over who should control the armed forces. The partisans of both sides naturally joined in the battle and, after two years of street violence and parliamentary turmoil, a group of obscure army colonels seized control of the country.

Helen Vlachos, whose opposition to the new military regime was to earn her almost three months under house arrest, has given a vivid account of Athens during the first eerie hours of the takeover: "Armed soldiers and officers had appeared and they formed cordons, stopping cars and pedestrians. Armoured cars were pouring into the central streets, filling the night with metallic, clanging echoes. Angry civilians were getting involved in noisy incidents, and drivers, suddenly confronted with closed streets, were sounding their horns in strident chorus. Harsh, brief commands given by the military were interrupted by shrill voices asking what it was all about.

"There was an oddity in this change in the character of the familiar city noises. Everything sounded wrong and artificial, as if the sound track of a war film had got itself mixed up with a documentary of night life in a peaceful city. We saw tanks, heavy, ambling monsters covered with mud, take up positions in front of the Ministry of Foreign Affairs, and soldiers jump from the turrets and go straight towards the policeman who was standing at the entrance and take over his place. 'Are they Greek . . . ?' I asked my husband, idiotically. 'Of course they are Greek,' he answered. 'What else can they be?' Of course."

Declaring its adherence to the traditional values of "Hellenic Christian civilization", the Colonels prorogued parliament, forbade political activities and arrested all those who were thought likely to raise objections. In addition to the hundreds of people taken into custody on the mainland, some 6,000 "dissidents" were rounded up and shipped off to primitive detention camps on the Aegean island of Yioura.

But after two years of political anarchy the prevailing mood of the country was one of relief rather than resistance. Strolling around Athens on the day after the coup, Mrs. Vlachos found that people "did not show any kind of concern, did not seem to care one way or the other. It was not a victory for anybody, man or party; it was an all-round defeat for all politicians of all denominations, a philosophically accepted overthrow of a situation that evidently did not appeal to the majority. 'Let them have a go' was the feeling of the day."

This feeling soon vanished, however, as the Colonels extended and consolidated the bleak apparatus of tyranny. Newspapers were submitted

The People's Puppet

Perhaps the most cheerful arenas of political expression in Athens are the city's open-air shadow theatres, where puppets traditionally act out a hilarious struggle between rulers and the ruled. These theatres are generally one-man shows that have been passed down from father to son for several generations. The puppeteer makes his own figures out of goatskin and cardboard, and, with the aid of long rods, manipulates them against a translucent screen, playing all the parts himself and often injecting topical political references into the dialogue.

Most of the plays are set in the period of Turkish occupation and recount the adventures of a downtrodden but rebellious little puppet named Karagiozis, who has huge bare feet, a hunchback and a bulbous nose. His one great asset is his right arm— five times longer than his left—which he uses to feed his insatiable appetite and to belabour his Turkish enemies. He also outsmarts his foes by boasting, lying, cheating and stealing. Despite his many faults, Greek audiences clearly identify with this curious cavalier's crusade against authority, and children shout warnings when he is in danger.

The shadow theatre had its golden age in the decade before the Second World War, when there were as many as 100 touring puppeteers. Today, the entertainment has to compete against films and television, and only a few puppeteers are left in Athens. But the saga of the roguish Karagiozis still attracts large crowds in the surviving theatres, and social historians recognize the puppet character as the hero of a living folk legend, embodying the humorous spirit of the Greek people in the face of oppression.

Behind the scenes, a puppeteer dangles the underdog hero Karagiozis, while a Turk waits on a chair.

During the show, the puppeteer (background) manipulates the characters on the screen and creates their voices, while a young assistant positions another puppet for its entrance. The assistants also do the sound effects.

At dusk, a mesmerized audience watches a shadow-play employing a typical setting: the tumbledown shanty belonging to Karagiozis leans in at the left side of the screen and the Turkish pasha's palace towers on the right.

In a characteristic imbroglio that will end well for Karagiozis, a fierce Turk overpowers the barefoot puppet patriot and threatens him with a cutlass.

to strict censorship and required to publish the Colonels' public relations handouts; the tragedies and comedies of the classical theatre were purged of dubious political references; civil servants, lawyers and teachers who stepped out of line were liable to summary dismissal; university students were required to take "loyalty" tests; long-haired boys and mini-skirted girls were condemned for "moral degeneracy". Even more sinister were the reports of torture inflicted on many of the regime's opponents.

In July, 1967, I had my first taste of Athens under the Colonels. Since my mission was to organize an association of Athenian alumni of Columbia University, I thought it best to steer clear of questions about the junta. As it turned out, my Athenian friends spoke of nothing else. Whatever their own political inclinations, they were united in denouncing the Colonels as betrayers of Greek freedom. One night a group of us went to a small *taverna* in Plaka and listened to a girl singing satirical songs about the Colonels. There was supposed to be a midnight ban on music in public places, and the songs themselves were forbidden by law; but look-outs posted in the streets warned us of approaching police. Baffled and embarrassed by the hostile silence, the three young officers beat a hasty retreat and almost immediately the whole *taverna* burst into one of the forbidden songs. The police, who were still within earshot, must have heard; but they did not return.

Ironically, it was the threat of renewed conflict with Turkey that freed Greece from dictatorship. The threat came in July, 1974, when the Colonels tried to seize Cyprus by engineering an abortive coup against Archbishop Makarios, the island's president. The Turkish Cypriot minority had been at loggerheads for years with the Greek Cypriot majority and the prospect of a takeover by Athens brought Turkish troops racing to the island. Unwilling to risk a full-scale war with Turkey, the Greek armed services chiefs not only refused to intervene on behalf of the Greek Cypriots but also told the junta to step aside and make way for a civilian government. After seven years of ruthless despotism, the Colonels had reached the end of the road.

The official news of their downfall was broadcast at 7 p.m. on July 23, 1974. By 8 o'clock more than 50,000 delirious Athenians had crowded into Syntagma Square to celebrate the return of democracy. According to one eye-witness account, "they raised their fingers in the sign of a V and began shouting, 'Victory for the people'. More and more people swarmed over the square, exploding into cheers and chants of hysterical cele-bration. Soon the sea of humanity—which by now had passed the 100,000 mark—overflowed into the streets, paralyzing the traffic. Blue and white Greek flags appeared out of nowhere and a brisk business was done by anyone who could furnish the hysterical crowd with flags or pictures of political leaders. As the joyful procession passed the Metropolis, the city's cathedral, an enterprising priest came out selling candles. Then, as night enveloped the scene, the flickering of thousands of candles danced among the crowd."

Constantine Karamanlis, who had served as prime minister during the years of tranquillity, agreed to head a Government of National Unity and in November his New Democracy Party swept to victory in the first Greek elections to be held for a decade. King Constantine, who had gone into exile in 1967 after leading an unsuccessful coup of his own, aroused rather less enthusiasm. For eight months he had allowed the Colonels to act in his name and in December, 1974, the Greeks voted by more than two to one to abolish the monarchy.

For all the high passions of the drama, the plot could hardly have been more familiar—a junta in and out of power, a king riding high one moment and stripped of his throne the next, a democratic government making a fresh start in the sure knowledge that critics would be hungry for its blood in no time at all. The tale of political turmoil had been repeating itself not just since the attainment of independence but ever since the emergence of Athens as a powerful city-state three millennia ago. It had been an old, old story by the time the Roman orator Cicero visited Athens as a young man in 92 B.C. and complained of "the rashness of the popular assemblies" and of the *levitas* (fickleness) of Athenians in exiling so many outstanding politicians whom they praised to the skies and then came to despise. More than 2,000 years after Cicero delivered that harsh judgment, Constantine Karamanlis made the same point—all the more powerfully for his being a potential victim of that *levitas*: "In our day there are no Messiahs; and if by chance we think we have found one, it will not be long before we turn on him. So we Greeks have been since ancient times. We are skilful at making idols, not that we may worship them, but that we may have the pleasure of destroying them."

A Lingering Village Spirit

Accompanied by her cat, an old widow makes her way along a sunny lane in Anaphiotika. Following tradition, she has worn black ever since her husband died.

Athens is among the most relentlessly modern of cities, but two of its districts—Anaphiotika and Kaisariani—seem no less dogged in their retention of a village atmosphere. Anaphiotika, sprawled on a bluff of the Acropolis overlooking the Plaka, was settled in the mid-19th Century by stonemasons brought from the Cyclades islands to help raise a new, post-Independence Athens. Kaisariani, lying six miles to the south-east amid a sea of new apartment blocks, was constructed by the government in 1923 to shelter Greeks forced out of Asia Minor at the end of the Turkish War. In both communities, amenities are primitive —Kaisariani has no adequate sewer system—and young people tend to seek more up-to-date housing. But older residents hold fast to village virtues, and in these unhurried streets the bustling metropolis seems light years away.

Rooftops form a haphazard design in Anaphiotika, whose founders often built houses in a day, thus winning title to the sites under Greek law.

In Kaisariani, a standpipe in the street provides a communal water supply.

A mother and son watch the world from the portals of their Kaisariani home.

Armed with broom, dustpan and bin, a street cleaner in Anaphiotika approaches a motorcycle — better suited than cars to the steep, crooked streets of the area.

A crudely constructed fence marking off the limits of a tiny garden area gets its annual facelifting of whitewash from a property-proud Kaisariani housewife.

As in Cycladic island villages, the people of Anaphiotika have enlivened their district's walls and sidewalks with coats of boldly coloured paint.

Out of the midday sun, a group of friends conduct a lively discussion beneath an olive tree in a courtyard branching off one of Kaisariani's many narrow alleys.

An oil lamp burns before religious articles arrayed in a bedroom corner.

Citadels of Tradition

In the predominantly working-class communities of Anaphiotika and Kaisariani, the homes are simply furnished, the political sentiments tend to be conservative, and the influence of the Greek Orthodox Church remains strong. Many homes have small shrines of holy images where a pious householder may burn incense and say prayers several times a day.

An Anaphiotika resident studies newspaper cartoons in a living room dominated by a portrait of a son who died of starvation during the Second World War.

On their Acropolis perch, the jumbled houses of Anaphiotika fade to greyness as the sun sinks behind the misty Parnes mountains, 12 miles to the north-west.

Bibliography

Andrewes, A., *The Greek Tyrants.* Hutchinson University Library, London, 1974.
Andrews, Kevin, *Cities of the World: Athens.* Phoenix House, London, 1967.
Antoniou, Jim, *Plaka.* Lycabettus Press, Athens, 1973.
Bowra, C. M., *Periclean Athens.* Weidenfeld and Nicolson, London, 1971.
Brain, Robert, *Friends and Lovers.* Hart-Davis, MacGibbon Ltd., London, 1976.
Burn, A. R., *The Pelican History of Greece.* Penguin Books Ltd., Harmondsworth, Middlesex, 1974.
Butterworth, Katharine, and Schneider, Sara, *Rebetika.* Komboloi, Athens, 1975.
Campbell, John, and Sherrard, Philip, *Modern Greece.* Ernest Benn Ltd., London, 1968.
Carey, J. P., and Carey, A. G., *The Web of Modern Greek Politics.* Columbia University Press, New York, 1968.
Clogg, Richard (ed.), *The Struggle for Greek Independence.* Macmillan Press Ltd., London, 1973.
Clogg, Richard, and Yannopoulos, George, *Greece under Military Rule.* Secker and Warburg, London, 1972.
Cook, Robert and Kathleen, *Southern Greece: An Archaeological Guide.* Faber and Faber Ltd., London, 1968.

Dakin, Douglas, *The Greek Struggle for Independence.* B. T. Batsford Ltd., London, 1973.
Dicks, T. R. B., *The Greeks.* David & Charles, Newton Abbot, Devon, 1972.
Eddy, Charles B., *Greece and the Greek Refugees.* George Allen & Unwin Ltd., London, 1931.
Fekete, Irene, *Athens.* Lutterworth Press, London, 1966.
Finer, Leslie, *Passport to Greece.* Longmans, Green and Co. Ltd., London, 1964.
Fodor, Eugene (ed.), *Fodor's Guide to Greece.* Hodder and Stoughton, London, 1977.
Foreign Area Studies, The American University, *Area Handbook for Greece.* U.S. Government Printing Office, Washington, D.C., 1970.
Gage, Nicholas, *Portrait of Greece.* American Heritage, New York, 1971.
Genevoix, Maurice, *The Greece of Karamanlis.* Doric Publications, London, 1973.
Hachette World Guides, *Athens and Environs.* Paris, 1962.
Holden, David, *Greece Without Columns.* Faber and Faber Ltd., London, 1972.
Holst, Gail, *Road to Rembetika.* Anglo-Hellenic Publishing, Athens, 1975.
King, Francis (ed.), *Introducing Greece.*

Methuen and Co. Ltd., London, 1956.
Lancaster, Osbert, *Classical Landscape With Figures.* John Murray, London, 1975.
Littman, Robert J., *The Greek Experiment.* Thames and Hudson, London, 1974.
Mead, Robin, *Greece.* B. T. Batsford Ltd., London, 1976.
Megas, G. A., *Greek Calendar Customs.* B. & M. Rhodis, Athens, 1963.
Miller, W., *Greek Life in Town and Country.* George Newnes, London, 1905.
O'Ballance, Edgar, *The Greek Civil War, 1944-49.* Faber and Faber Ltd., London, 1966.
Papandreou, Andreas, *Democracy at Gunpoint: The Greek Front.* André Deutsch, London, 1971.
Radice, Betty (ed.), *Who's Who in the Ancient World.* Penguin Books Ltd., Harmondsworth, Middlesex, 1975.
Rinvolucri, Mario, *Anatomy of a Church.* Burns and Oates, London, 1966.
Schoder, Raymond, *Ancient Greece from the Air.* Thames and Hudson, London, 1974.
Theodorakis, Mikis, *Journals of Resistance.* Hart-Davis MacGibbon, London, 1973.
Travlos, John, *Pictorial Dictionary of Ancient Athens.* Thames and Hudson, London, 1971.
Woodhouse, C. M., *The Story of Modern Greece.* Faber and Faber Ltd., London, 1968.

Acknowledgements and Picture Credits

The editors wish to thank the following for their valuable assistance: Professor J. P. Baron, King's College, London; Charles Dettmer, Thames Ditton, Surrey; Susan Goldblatt, London; Mike Kallas, Athens; National Tourist Office of Greece, London; Elizabeth Micheli, Athens; Frances Middlestorb, London; Karin Pearce, London; Press and Information Office, Greek Embassy, London; David Sinclair, London; Mary Staples, London; Marguerite Tarrant, London; Colin Thubron, London; Helen Vlachos, Athens; Giles Wordsworth, London.

Page 88, Song, *"This Alien Life"* by Apostolos Kaldaras, reproduced by courtesy of Elias Petropoulos. Quotations on pages 17 and 19 reproduced by courtesy of *The Geographical Magazine,* London. Quotations on pages 13, 169 and 172 reproduced by permission of A. D. Peters & Co. Ltd. Quotation on pages 177-8 from *Classical Landscape With Figures* by Osbert Lancaster reproduced by permission of John Murray (Publishers) Ltd. Quotation on page 180 from *House Arrest* by Helen Vlachos, published 1971, reproduced by permission of Andre Deutsch Ltd. Quotation on pages 184-5 extracted from *The Greek Upheaval* by Taki Theodora-

copulos reproduced by permission of Stacey International, London, 1976. Quotations on pages 165, 172-3 from *Greek Life in Town and Country* by W. Miller, published by George Newnes, 1905. Quotations on pages 173, 174 and 179 from *Greece Without Columns* by David Holden, published 1972, reproduced by permission of Faber and Faber Ltd.

Sources for pictures in this book are shown below, with the exception of those already credited. Credits for pictures from left to right are separated by commas: from top to bottom by dashes.
Cover—Michael Freeman. Front end paper—Constantine Manos. 4—Michael Freeman. 7—Constantine Manos. 9—Michael Freeman. 10, 11—Map by Hunting Surveys Ltd., London. Silhouettes by Norman Bancroft-Hunt. 12, 13—Michael Freeman. 16 to 22—Constantine Manos. 23—Michael Freeman. 24 to 26—Constantine Manos. 27—Michael Freeman. 28—Constantine Manos, Michael Freeman, Michael Freeman, Constantine Manos. 29—Constantine Manos. 30—Michael Freeman. 31—Michael Freeman, Constantine Manos, Constantine Manos, Michael Freeman. 32, 33—Constantine Manos. 34—Scala, Florence. 38, 39—Michael Freeman. 41—Drawing by Norman Bancroft-Hunt. 42 to 47—

Constantine Manos. 49—Michael Freeman. 51 to 55—Constantine Manos. 57—Paul Popper Ltd., London. 58, 59—Bildarchiv Preussischer Kulturbesitz. 60—Fotomas Index (John Freeman). 61—National Portrait Gallery, London. 70, 73—Constantine Manos. 74, 75—Michael Freeman. 76 to 79—Constantine Manos. 81—Bob Davies, Aspect Picture Library, London. 85 to 89—Constantine Manos. 92, 93—Michael Freeman. 94—Constantine Manos. 95, 96—Michael Freeman. 97—Constantine Manos, Michael Freeman. 98, 99—Michael Freeman. 100, 101—Constantine Manos. 102—Michael Freeman. 104 to 107—Constantine Manos. 110—Michael Freeman. 111 to 137—Constantine Manos. 139—Michael Freeman. 140, 141—Michael Holford. 142, 143—Benaki Museum, Athens. 145—Michael Freeman. 146—Michael Freeman, Constantine Manos. 147—Constantine Manos. 148—Michael Freeman. 150—Constantine Manos. 152 to 156—Michael Freeman. 157 to 167—Constantine Manos. 170, 171—Royal Collection, Windsor. 173, 175—Constantine Manos. 179—Camera Press Ltd., London. 181 to 187—Michael Freeman. 188—Constantine Manos. 189, 190—Michael Freeman. 191—Constantine Manos. 192 to 197, last end paper—Michael Freeman.

Index

Numerals in italics indicate a photograph or drawing of the subject mentioned.

Colour reproduction by Irwin Photography Ltd., at their Leeds PDI Scanner Studio.
Filmsetting by C. E. Dawkins (Typesetters) Ltd., London, SE1 1UN.
Printed and bound in Italy by Arnoldo Mondadori, Verona.